The Book of Days

A resource book of activities for special days in the year

Adrian Wallwork

CAMBRIDGE
UNIVERSITY PRESS

CAMBRIDGE UNIVERSITY PRESS
Cambridge, New York, Melbourne, Madrid, Cape Town,
Singapore, São Paulo, Delhi, Mexico City

Cambridge University Press
The Edinburgh Building, Cambridge CB2 8RU, UK

www.cambridge.org
Information on this title: www.cambridge.org/elt/ccc

First published 2013
Reprinted 2013

Printed in the United Kingdom by Short Run Press, Exeter

A catalogue record for this publication is available from the British Library

ISBN 978-1-107-68570-3 Paperback with Audio CDs (2)

Cambridge University Press has no responsibility for the persistence or
accuracy of URLs for external or third-party internet websites referred to in
this publication, and does not guarantee that any content on such websites is,
or will remain, accurate or appropriate. Information regarding prices, travel
timetables and other factual information given in this work is correct at
the time of first printing but Cambridge University Press does not guarantee
the accuracy of such information thereafter.

Contents

Acknowledgements

This book is dedicated to my mother, Jean Wallwork, and my father, Basil Wallwork, whose constant faith, encouragement and love have been a great support for me.

I would like to thank the following people who arranged interviews for me or provided materials from their personal archives:
Dr Enrico Frontini, Francesca Tolaini, Wayne Burge, all the Muslims at the Muslim Centre in Pisa, the children from various primary and secondary schools in Hale, Cheshire, England, Sue Redford, Heather Walton (Language Centre), Andrea Conrad and Au Pairs Direct. Very special thanks to Chris Hayes of the International Society in Manchester. Thanks to all at List SpA and International House Pisa, especially Chris Powell and Seeme Faiyaz, and to these students: Antonella Giani, Stefano Chessa, Giuseppe Amato, Olaf Bouermeister, Maria Turchetto, Matteo Gorini, Mariuccia Coviello, Domenico Coviello, Carina Bendrame.

A very big thanks to Alyson Maskell for considerably improving the manuscript and to Nóirín Burke at Cambridge University Press for all her patience. Thanks also to the following piloters:
Claire Bradshaw, Internexus, London, UK; Michaela Canková, Prague, Czech Republic; Julian Child, The British Council, Bilbao, Spain; Maria Edvirgem Zeny, SBCI Curitiba, Curitiba, Brazil; Juan Felix Garcia, Ministry of Education, La Habana, Cuba; Leigh Fergus, Gervais, France; Amy King, Yonsei University, Seoul, Korea; Geraldine Mark, Cheltenham, UK; Clare McGinn, Belgrade, Yugoslavia; Nicholas Shaw, Cambridge English Studies, La Coruña, Spain; Mark Thompson, King's College of English, Bangkok, Thailand.

A sincere thanks to the following people (some of whose surnames I never discovered) who agreed to talk in front of my microphone on the streets, in public libraries, in their homes, at their schools, at work, in their ethnic centres and at their universities. Many of them contributed to what has been the most enlightening and religious period of my life (not bad for an atheist!). Those who also invited me to witness their religious ceremonies and to share their convictions (and wonderful food!) deserve a special mention:
Mohamed Sultan (Afghanistan), Aouadi Nadjet (Algeria), Carina Bendrame, Deborah Longobardi (Argentina), Tom Southern (Australia), Susie (Austria), Momem Ahmed (Bangladesh), Beatrice Patry (Belgium), Prof. Marcos Tognon, Paulo Spartani de Godoy (Brazil), Shelley Thomas (Canada), Lenka Siroky (Czech Republic), Jaime Fuller (Chile), Prof. Ve Chang Lu (China), Zana Gugurevic (Croatia), Lina Thorgaard (Denmark), Mohamed Hammad (Egypt), Sgt J Bradwell, Alastair Brogdon, Andrew Brogdon, Stephen Brogdon, Gillian Brogdon, Marc Ferster, Anne Ray, Anna Southern, Hayley Wallwork, Stuart Wallwork (England), Pipsa Manninen, Pirso Päivikki (Finland), Isabel Vanprays (France), Peter Erhard, Ina Harloff, Hans Luebke, Nicole Schulze, Eberhard Steiger (Germany), Dorothea Dodson (Ghana), Efterpi Kokkimou (Greece), Sandra (Holland), Annamaria Filep, Tamas Bartha (Hungary), Asgeir Sigfusdottir (Iceland), Biman Bandyopadhyay, Pew Bose (India), Dewi Chandrasa, Pujiati Sri Lestari (Indonesia), Sorayah Parsi (Iran), Niall O'Cuilinn (Irish Republic), Andreina Marchesi, Tommaso Wallwork (Italy), Noriko Fujioka, Yoshie Kojima, Masako Komai, Yukari Saito, Midori Yamamoto (Japan), Maurice Makau (Kenya), Suad M Abushah (Libya), Claudia Cano (Mexico), Karim Ouatmane (Morocco), Gunn-Marit Øygarden, Britt Kari Kalhagen (Norway), Seeme Faiyaz (Pakistan), Mohamed Khalil (Palestine), Stanislas Zaleski (Poland), Lucia Oliveira Noversa (Portugal), Eugenie Hupar, Janna Mesko (Russian Federation), Hanadi Shebab (Saudi Arabia), Mohamed Aly Sow, Maodo Sylla (Senegal), Rebecca Tan Ching Kiang (Singapore), Michaela Jelinkovà, Monika Karulovà (Slovakia), Vesna Opacic (Slovenia), Honor Routledge (South Africa), Bum-Soo Elin, Park Mu Yob (South Korea), Vanessa Fernández Méndez (Spain), Muna Zunoon (Sudan), Patrizia Rigobon (Switzerland), Li-Ying Chen (Taiwan), Ganpoebaro Ginpa (Tibet), Reyhan Bazaran, Aliye Gungor (Turkey), Marcheline Acayo (Uganda), Elder R Andrew Crane, Pete Forster, Natashia Hancock, Lieutenant Nate Hancock, Sean Hancock, Elder Matthew Kober, Morgan Moody, Major Howard Weant (USA), Ngo Dai Len (Vietnam), Nancy Nuttall (Wales).

The author and publisher are grateful to the following for permission to use copyright material in The Book of Days. While every effort has been made, it has not been possible to identify the sources of all the material used and in such cases the publishers would welcome information from the copyright owners:

Eric Lee and the IFWEA for the extract on p. 25 from 'International Women's Day', Worker's Education No. 7, Dec. 1994; Tania Tsimaba Bueya and Ling Tai for the extracts on p. 29 from To The World's Best Mother, edited by Helen Exley. Reprinted by permission of Exley Publications Ltd.; the quote at the end of p. 45 is an extract by Aysegul Corecki from To Dad, published by Exley Publications Ltd. Copyright 1976, 1990 Richard and Helen Exley. Used with permission; 'Sun' on p. 47 is by Elaine Antone, published in When it rains: Papago and Pima Poetry, ed. Ofelia Zepeda, the University of Arizona Press; 'What is the Sun?' is by Miss J.A. Haywood, from Over the Moon Cheshire, published by 'Poetry Now Young Writers'; thanks to Stanley Thornes Publishers for the extract on p. 50, col. 2 from Key History for Key Stage 3, The Twentieth Century World by Neil de Marco and Richard Radway; Music Sales Limited for 'War' on p. 75, words and music by Allen Cole & Carlton Barrett, © Copyright 1976 Bob Marley Music Limited, Blue Mountain Music Limited, 8 Kensington Park Road, London W11. Used by permission of Music Sales Limited. All rights reserved. International Copyright Secured; Kynan Ellen and Sophie Hopgood for the letters on p. 87; Little Brown and Company for the extracts on pp. 90 and 95 from Birthdays by Linda Rannells Lewis; 'Relate' for permission to reproduce the information on p. 101 about causes of marital discord; on p. 108 'The ancestors have spoken today' is by Okot p'Bitek, Uganda, from Horn of My Love, published by East African Educational Publishers Limited; 'For Joe Mackinaw', 'The Past' and 'Untitled' are from Adam Shoemaker, Black Words White Page: Aboriginal Literature 1929–1988, University of Queensland Press, 1989.

The recording of the extract from Martin Luther King's speech on August 28, 1963 (words on p. 15) was taken from Great Speeches of the Twentieth Century under license from PolyMedia, a Division of PolyGram Group Distribution, Inc.

Photographs by:
©BBC p. 35; Corbis-Bettmann pp. 15 (UPI/drinking fountain), 25 (Reuters/Naomi Campbell, Everett/Madonna, Reuters/ Mother Theresa, Eva Peron), 39 (Robert Maass/maypole); Imperial War Museum p. 77; Katz Pictures pp. 25 (Simon Townsley/Margaret Thatcher), 95 (Tom Stoddart/Bar Mitzvah); Magnum Photos pp. 15 (Bob Adelman/Martin Luther King), 33 (Abbas/crucifixion), 61 (Bruno Barbey), 71 (cemetery), 75 (Jean Gaumy); Panos Pictures p. 95 (Crispin Hughes/Akot); Popperfoto Ltd pp. 15 (funeral), 21 (carnival), 25 (Princess Diana); Rex Features Ltd p. 15 (Nobel Prize); Tony Stone Images pp. 81 (Thanksgiving), 95 (Myrleen Cate/holy communion), 97 (Bob Thomas), 101 (Susan Vogel); Telegraph Colour Library p. 65 (VCL/UN Logo); Topham Picturepoint pp. 15 (fire), 39 (parade).

Picture research by Diane Jones

Sound recordings by James Richardson at Studio AVP, London

Produced by Gecko Limited, Bicester, Oxon

Illustrations by Jane Cape, Alastair Gray, David Mitcheson, Chris Molan, Tracy Rich, Jamie Sneddon and Ian West.

Cover illustration by Elaine Cox

Map of *The Book of Days*

Exercise   T = especially suited for teenagers, but generally suitable for adults too

Level   lower = low intermediate and above

           mid = intermediate

           upper = upper intermediate and above

Skills   L = listening   R = short text reading   Q = quiz   S = discussion   W = writing

Day	Date	Exercise	Level	Time	Skills
1 New Year's Day	Jan 1 (most countries)	**1** New Year celebrations **2** Resolutions (T) **3** Which New Year?	mid mid mid	20 mins 15 mins 15 mins	S, R, L L, S L
2 Martin Luther King Jr's Birthday	Jan 15 (US)	**1** Martin Luther King Jr's life (T) **2** I have a dream (T)	mid mid	15 mins 15 mins	L R, L
3 Valentine's Day	Feb 14 (US, UK, some others)	**1** Who was St Valentine? (T) **2** How do you celebrate ...? (T) **3** Valentine's messages **4** How romantic are you? (T) **5** Friends' Day (T)	lower lower mid mid mid	10 mins 10 mins 10 mins 10 mins 20 mins	L R, S R, W Q, S Q, L, S
4 Carnival	varies	**1** Carnival quiz (T) **2** Carnival in Brazil	mid mid	20 mins 10 mins	Q, S, L R
5 Fasting	varies	**1** Lent **2** Yom Kippur **3** Ramadan	upper upper upper	10 mins 10 mins 15 mins	R, S R, S R, L
6 Women's Day	March 8	**1** Women, work and politics **2** Whose liberation? **3** F, N or M?	mid upper lower	20 mins 25 mins 15 mins	S, Q Q, L, S dictation, S
7 Mother's Day	varies	**1** Mummy, mom, mama **2** Fact file (T)	lower/upper upper	15 mins 15 mins	L, L R, S
8 Easter	March/April	**1** Easter traditions **2** Easter quiz **3** The Crucifixion **4** The Holy Bible	mid lower upper mid	15 mins 5 mins 15 mins 10 mins	R, S, L Q L, S R, S
9 April Fools' Day	April 1	**1** All Fools' Day (T) **2** You can't fool me (T)	mid mid	20 mins 20 mins	R, L R, L, S
10 May 1	May 1	**1** International Labour Day **2** May Day (T)	mid mid	15 mins 10 mins	R, L, S R, S
11 Buddha's Birthday	varies	Elements of Buddhism	upper	25 mins	R, L, S
12 Children's Day	varies	Boys and girls (T)	mid	25 mins	R, L, S
13 Father's Day	varies	**1** Father and son (T) **2** Father's Day quiz (T)	mid mid	15 mins 25 mins	R, L, S Q, L, S
14 Summer Solstice	June 21 (Dec 21)	**1** Sun poems **2** Sun quiz	mid mid	20 mins 20 mins	W, R S, Q, L

15 Independence Day	July 4 (US)	**1** When and who from? (T) **2** July 4 (T) **3** India (T)	mid mid mid	15 mins 15 mins 10 mins	L, S S, R, L R, L
16 Diwali	Oct/Nov (India)	**1** Diwali **2** Hinduism	mid upper	5 mins 30 mins	R R, L, S
17 Reunification Day	Oct 3 (Germany)	**1** The Berlin Wall (T) **2** The good old days? (T)	upper upper	15 mins 25 mins	R, L R, S
18 Teachers' Day	varies, Oct 5 World Teachers' Day	**1** Great teachers (T) **2** My (ideal) English teacher is ... (T) **3** We don't need no education (T) **4** Students' days	lower lower lower upper	10 mins 15 mins 15 mins 10 mins	R L, Q Q, L, S R, S
19 Columbus Day	Oct 12	**1** History quiz (T) **2** Americans	lower mid	20 mins 15 mins	L, S S
20 United Nations' Day	Oct 24	**1** United Nations – facts and figures **2** Budget allocation	mid mid	20 mins 15 mins	R, L, S S
21 Halloween	Oct 31	**1** Past and present (T) **2** Halloween celebrations (T) **3** The supernatural (T)	mid mid mid	20 mins 15 mins 10 mins	R Q, L S
22 Day of the Dead	varies	**1** Remembering the dead **2** Songs for our ancestors	upper upper	15 mins 15 mins	R, S L
23 Guy Fawkes' Night	Nov 5 (UK)	The Gunpowder Plot (T)	upper	20 mins	R, L
24 Remembrance Day	Nov 11	**1** 'Greater love ...' (T) **2** War **3** Why join the army? **4** Conscious	mid mid upper upper	15 mins 15 mins 15 mins 20 mins	L, S, R R, S L, S R, S, L
25 Thanksgiving	4th Thursday in Nov (US)	**1** The Mayflower (T) **2** Rewriting history? **3** A generation later ...	mid upper upper	15 mins 10 mins 15 mins	R, L L R, S
26 Winter Solstice	Dec 21 (June 21)	**1** The shortest day **2** Mithras and Yuletide	lower upper	10 mins 15 mins	S R, L
27 Christmas	Dec 25	**1** Christmas origins **2** Christmas scene (T) **3** Christmas quiz (T) **4** Santa Claus (T) **5** Christmas games (T)	upper mid mid mid mid	5 mins 15 mins 10 mins 15 mins 30 mins	R S, L Q, L R, L, S games
28 Birthdays	varies	**1** Your birth and the zodiac **2** Birthday parties (T) **3** Stages of life (T) **4** Names **5** Rites of passage (T)	mid mid mid upper upper	15 mins 15 mins 20 mins 10 mins 15 mins	S, L L, S Q, L, S R, S R, L, S
29 Wedding Day	varies	**1** Ancient and modern **2** Wedding customs **3** Words of wisdom? **4** Some statistics **5** For better or for worse?	upper mid upper upper upper	25 mins 10 mins 10 mins 20 mins 15 mins	R, L, S L R L, S S
30 Days of the Week	varies	**1** Markets, gods and planets **2** The Sabbath **3** Thank God it's Friday	upper upper upper	10 mins 15 mins 20 mins	R L S

Teacher's Introduction

Rationale

The philosophy of this book is to get students curious about particular traditions and religious events. It is designed to draw on learners' own experiences, knowledge, opinions and feelings, and thus provoke lively discussion on how, where and why these days are celebrated.

These are one-off supplementary skills lessons, whose prime aim is to inform and entertain, in a language which just happens to be English.

Level and age

The book is aimed at teenagers and young adults. Most exercises are pitched at a mid to upper intermediate level.

When to use

The order in which the Days appear in the Contents generally coincides with a typical calendar from the UK. Most activities don't have to be used on the Day in question, e.g. discussion on Buddhism ostensibly should be on Buddha's Birthday (Day 11), but it doesn't have to be. In any case, most lessons move from an initial look at the festival in question to a broader discussion of its implications. You can also link topics together, i.e. a discussion on Buddhism might lead into one on Hinduism (Day 16). The lesson on Valentine's Day (Day 3) could lead to talk of Weddings (Day 29). Teachers' Day has been fixed on October 5, simply because this is World Teachers' Day, but that was a very arbitrary choice and you may find, for example, that in the country where you are teaching there is a local Teachers' Day.

Students' Pages

The Students' Pages are designed to get away from the typical ELT Students' Page, i.e. there are very few rubrics. Because the book is multi-level, it is up to you, the teacher, to exploit the passages and pictures as you wish. They can be legally photocopied.

Teacher's Notes

On the Teacher's Pages each unit is introduced with a panel containing the following items:

Date: suggests when to use the unit. However, many units are not tied to one particular day and can be used whenever seems suitable.

Level and **age:** tells you approximately what level and age of students the exercises are suitable for. The level indicated is the minimum level, which means that any exercise indicated as suitable for intermediate will generally also be suitable for upper intermediate, advanced and proficiency students too, since the majority of exercises are discussions, which are really level independent.

Time: tells you how long each exercise will last. This is the minimum time for doing the exercise on the Students' Page plus the related listening. It does not include time taken for pre-teaching vocabulary nor for any extra activities (follow-ups, songs, etc.). Exercise length really depends on how interested you and your students are in the subject in question.

Grammar: indicates any grammatical structures that occur frequently in an exercise. However there are no grammar exercises as such.

Advice: warns of possible problems due to cultural differences, and political, religious and sexual ideas. Be sensitive to your students' beliefs. Also, remember that some exercises will only work if students have an informed opinion on the subject.

Vocabulary: indicates some of the vocabulary items your students may have difficulty with.

The Teacher's Notes then continue as follows:

Background information ℹ️

This information is not essential in your preparation of the lesson. I hope you find it interesting, and you may wish to pass some of it on to your students so that you yourself can become a resource for your students. However, if you are in a hurry to prepare your lesson, skip it.

Instructions

These contain ideas on how to exploit the information on the Students' Pages. They are only ideas, not constrictions, and are generally flexible enough for you to play around with as you wish. This book is intended primarily to promote discussion, as students compare their festivals, faiths and opinions.

Even in monolingual groups you will find that each region, village, family has its own traditions. At the beginning of each lesson, find out from students what they know about the festival in question, then they will be more motivated to listen or read to find out the details. Use the illustrations and the texts on the Students' Pages as a stimulus for getting students to write down related questions, which they can then try to answer together.

Listening 📼

All the listening exercises are outlined on the Teacher's Page, very few on the Students' Page. This means you are free to do the ones you want. The question of level is critical here. Many of the listenings are authentic, with all the pros and cons which go with such recordings. But just because the listening may seem difficult, it doesn't mean the task has to be. Many listening exercises have comprehension questions. You can either write these on the board or OHP, or simply dictate them. The questions are suggestions only, you can make up your own questions to suit the level and knowledge of your students.

Cover illustration by Elaine Cox

Some of the recordings are authentic (i.e. ones I recorded myself), or improvised (i.e. actors in a studio talking about their own personal experiences or opinions). These are generally harder to follow than the scripted recordings but are obviously useful exercises in listening to authentic speech. The scripted recordings were all made in a professional recording studio. The simulated radio talk shows are based on recordings I made with people from all parts of the world. Please note that in the studio recordings none of the actors used false accents – this means that all the Indian, Scottish, Australian, New Zealand, Canadian, English, Irish and American accents you hear are the real thing! Honestly!

Key 🔑

Keys are given for all exercises, where appropriate.

Follow-up

These are ideas for follow-up activities. You should also encourage students to use encyclopaedias, CD ROMs and the World Wide Web.

Songs and Films

These are very subjective suggestions for songs and films that tie in with the subject in hand. Students may have their own ideas for songs they might like to bring in.

Reading and vocabulary

The book contains a lot of useful thematic vocabulary, e.g. on religion, politics and customs, but unavoidably there is also some rather specialist vocabulary, which, where possible, we have tried to illustrate, but which will in any case need to be pre-taught. The reading passages have been kept short and should be used as a springboard to discussion rather than as comprehension exercises. The passages themselves are either direct quotations from people I interviewed (i.e. those followed by names in parentheses) or amalgamations of what I read in my source books (see Bibliography on page 9).

Discussions A–Z

For any of you who happen to have *Discussions A–Z* (also part of the Cambridge Copy Collection) here are some useful links to exercises which you can use as follow-ups.

Day 2:   Colour (*Discussions A–Z Intermediate*)

Day 3:   Love (*Discussions A–Z Intermediate*)

Day 6:   Gender, Revolution (*Discussions A–Z Advanced*)

Day 8:   Origins (*Discussions A–Z Intermediate*)

Day 12: Kids (*Discussions A–Z Advanced*)

Day 13: Family (*Discussions A–Z Intermediate*)

Day 16: Class (*Discussions A–Z Advanced*)

Day 18: Schools (*Discussions A–Z Intermediate*)

Day 19: Xenophobia (*Discussions A–Z Intermediate*)

Day 20: X-certificate (*Discussions A–Z Advanced*)

Day 21: Beliefs (*Discussions A–Z Intermediate*)

Day 24: War (*Discussions A–Z Advanced*)

Day 25: Xenophobia (*Discussions A–Z Intermediate*)
Utopia (*Discussions A–Z Advanced*)

Day 28: You (*Discussions A–Z Advanced*)
Zodiac (*Discussions A–Z Advanced*)

Day 29: Family (*Discussions A–Z Intermediate*)

Mail me

Please send comments and notes of any inaccuracies or suggestions for future editions of this book to:
adrian @list.it

Bibliography

I am indebted to the authors of the books all of which I delved into to research *The Book of Days*. The dates refer to editions I used.

General books on festivals

Q. Cooper and P. Sullivan *Maypoles, Martyrs and Mayhem* Bloomsbury 1994

G. Palmer and N. Lloyd *A Year of Festivals* F. Wayne 1972

D. Carey and J. Large *Festivals Family and Food* Hawthorn Press Stroud 1982

F. Purton *Festivals and Celebrations* Basil Blackwell 1989

J.G. Walshe *Dates and Meanings of Religious and other Festivals* Foulsham Educational 1993

G. Sublette *The Book of Days* Berkley Publishing 1996

M. Ickis *The Book of Festivals and Holidays the World Over* Dodd, Mead & Company 1970

D. Spicer *The Book of Festivals* Gale Research Company 1969

A.M. Malcoc ed. *Celebrate! Holidays in the USA.* English Language Programs Division, USIA, Washington DC 1994

Religion and Fasting

Holy Bible Oxford University Press

W. Owen Cole ed. *Five World Faiths* Cassell 1991

T. Ware *The Orthodox Church* Penguin 1983

I. Wilson *Jesus the Evidence* Pan Books 1985

Larousse Gastronomique Paul Hamlyn 1991

R. Tannahill *Food in History* Penguin 1988

General reference, sources for statistics

Workers' Education, various numbers

R. Bailey *The True State of the Planet* The Free Press 1995

J. Boyden *Families* Gaia Books Limited 1993

The Guinness Book of Records Bantam Books 1996

Hutchinson Pocket Factfinder Helicon Publishing 1992

Ash *The Top 10 of Everything* Dorling Kindersley 1996

R. Tripp *International Thesaurus of Quotations* Penguin 1985

W. Farrel *The Myth of Male Power* Berkley Books 1996

N. DeMarco and R. Radway *The Twentieth Century World* Stanley Thornes 1995

Etymology

Oxford English Dictionary (full version) Oxford University Press

Webster's New World Dictionary, Third College Edition Prentice Hall 1991

W. Skeat *Concise Dictionary of English Etymology* Wordsworth Reference 1993

Brewers Dictionary of Phrase and Fable Cassell 1983

O. Pianigiani *Dizionario Etimologico della Lingua Italiana* I Dioscuri 1988

Dictionnaire Historique de la Langue Française Le Robert 1992

Etymologisches Wörterbuch des Deutschen dtv 1995

DAY 1 New Year's Day

Date	January 1 (different for some religions)
Level	intermediate
Age	all ages
Time	Ex 1 20–30 minutes
	Ex 2 15 minutes
	Ex 3 15 minutes
Grammar	Ex 2 *going to* for future intentions
Vocabulary	celebrate, greetings card, resolutions, give up, predictions, calendar, shrine, temple, spring, pocket money, lump of coal, disguise, Pope, Jewish, Druids

1 New Year celebrations

Listening 1

- Hand out photocopies and begin by playing the song *Auld Lang Syne* (roughly translated: for old times' sake). Find out if anyone has heard it before or recognises the tune. It is sung at midnight on Hogmanay, the Scottish last day of the year. Scotland celebrates New Year's Eve much more extensively than the rest of the UK. The version of the song sung today was made famous by the Scottish poet Robert Burns, though he was not the original author. When singing *Auld Lang Syne*, it is traditional for everyone to link arms in a circle, as in the illustration.

- Students then read the texts, and discuss what their New Year has in common with New Year in Iran and Vietnam, and whether the first day of spring might be a more sensible time for the New Year to begin.

Listening 2

- Students are going to hear a studio-recorded talk show, where the guest is a Scottish woman comparing the New Year in Scotland with New Year celebrations in China and Japan. Focus students' attention on the table. They can either answer the questions in relation to their own country, or, in preparation for listening, try and guess some of the answers for Scotland, China and Japan.

- Play the recording and point out that not all the table can be filled in.

	SCOTLAND	CHINA	JAPAN
1	Jan 1	varies	Jan 1
2	?	no – agricultural	yes (shrines/temples)
3	1 day	5 days	3 days
4	? (no, only at Christmas)	?	yes
5	?	?	?
6	first footing	pocket money new clothes	pocket money
7	?	?	?
8	?	?	yes
9	? (yes)	?	yes
10	*Auld Lang Syne*	?	ring a gong

A Welcome to *One World*, which tonight comes to you from Edinburgh in Scotland. First let me introduce our guest, Fiona Macdonald, who's going to be talking about New Years' Festivals in Japan and China. So do they have anything in common with what goes on here in Scotland?

B Well, in Scotland we only celebrate for one day, whereas in Japan they basically eat, drink and visit shrines for three days, and the Chinese have five days' national holiday.

A Five days? But not in January?

B The Japanese have the same calendar as us, so they start on January the first. But in China they use the lunar calendar, so it varies from year to year. It's actually called a *spring festival* and was the time when farmers and peasants used to rest physically and spiritually before sowing the seeds.

A I've heard that in Japan nearly everyone sends cards at New Year, whereas we generally send our cards at Christmas. Is that true of China too?

B I'm not sure that they do, actually. But one thing both countries have in common is that they give their children pocket money. Many Chinese also wear new clothes as a way of leaving behind the old year and all its misfortunes.

A So it's a kind of ritual to bring good luck?

B Of course in Scotland we have the tradition of 'first footing', you know, when the first person to visit your house in the New Year should be handsome and dark haired.

A And a man.

B Yes, not a woman, because in some communities they were thought to bring bad luck. And this man was supposed to bring a lump of coal, a lump of bread and a bottle of whisky.

A What about resolutions? This year I've decided to give up smoking, like I do almost every year. Do the Chinese and Japanese go in for this kind of thing?

B Not really, no, but they do make predictions for the future. For instance, at the Japanese shrines and temples you can find out your fortune from some little bits of paper. Then at 12 o'clock they ring a gong in a temple 108 times, to send away the 108 evil desires in the Buddhist religion.

DAY 1 New Year's Day

1 New Year celebrations

Auld Lang Syne

Should auld acquaintance be forgot,
and never brought to mind?
Should auld acquaintance be forgot,
and days o' lang syne?

For auld lang syne my dear,
for auld land syne:
We'll tak' a cup o' kindness yet,
for auld lang syne.

Then here's a hand my trusty fiere [1],
and gie's a hand o' thine.
We'll tak' a right guid-willie waught [2],
for auld lang syne.

For auld lang syne my dear,
for auld lang syne:
We'll tak' a cup o' kindness yet,
for auld lang syne.

Robert Burns

*Scots celebrate the
New Year by singing
Auld Lang Syne.*

[1] friend
[2] drink

New Year in Iran is called Nowruz and it always begins on the first day of spring. Nowruz celebrates the death of the old year and the rebirth of the new: Good versus Evil. A few weeks before the New Year, we clean our houses. We make new clothes and cook delicious foods. People disguise themselves with make-up, wear brightly coloured clothes, and sing and dance in the streets. We visit all our friends, and we send cards to those Iranians who live in other countries.

(Sorayah Parsi, Iran)

The Tet, our Vietnamese New Year, is the most important celebration in Vietnam. Many people are superstitious and we make predictions for the new year depending on what animal noise we hear first, or on who is the first person to visit our house. We light candles to our guardian gods and they make reports on us in heaven.

(Ngo Dai Len, Vietnam)

	Your country	Scotland	China	Japan
1 When is it?				
2 Is it a religious festival?				
3 How long do celebrations last?				
4 Do people send greetings cards?				
5 Is it a time for visiting relatives?				
6 What do people do to bring good luck?				
7 What typical foods are eaten?				
8 Do people dance/drink a lot?				
9 Do they make predictions or resolutions?				
10 What happens at midnight on New Year's Eve?				

2 Resolutions

- Tell students that in Britain people make resolutions on New Year's Eve about what they plan to do or give up in the coming year. Tell the class one of your own resolutions (e.g. This year I'm really going to listen when my children/husband/partner talk(s) to me).
- Hand out photocopies. Students first do the listening exercise and then answer the questions at the top of their page.

Listening 3

- Students hear four teenagers' resolutions for the New Year. They should simply note down what the resolutions are. After listening, elicit which construction is used to make resolutions – *going to*.

 Boy 1: give up chocolate;
Girl 1: be more organised;
Boy 2: stop lying to parents, and stop eating beefburgers;
Girl 2: give up junk food and eat more healthily.

A Well, I think this year I'm going to try and give up chocolate.
B Are you?
A Yeah, because I eat so much of it. And you know, it might make me fat or spotty or something, so I think I should, you know, see if I can give it up.
B I'd never be able to do that.
A What about you, what are you going to do?
B I'm definitely going to become more organised from 12 o'clock tonight, definitely.
A I'll believe that when I see it.
B It's true.
C I've got two. I'm going to try, the first one I'm going try and stop lying to my parents, because I'm constantly lying to them, all the time. And the second, I've got to stop eating beefburgers. [Why?] I can't stop eating them.
D I always I always find that I eat too much junk food and and like McDonald's and beefburgers and things like you say. I've got to start giving up that and eat more more healthily, and eat more fruit and vegetables and stuff like that. I always say I'm going to do that, never do.

3 Which New Year?

- In multinational groups ask students to discuss what system their calendar follows and when their New Year is.
- Focus attention on the calendar for October 1582. Ask students what they notice about it and get them to hypothesise on what happened to the missing ten days. Then do the listening task.

Listening 4

Students hear an explanation for October 1582. They also hear about the different days on which New Year has been celebrated in England, and, finally, about when different countries adopted the Gregorian Calendar.

2 Druid Nov 1, Anglo-Saxon Dec 25, Middle Ages Mar 25
3 England 1752, Greece 1923, Russia 1918, Scotland 1600
4 Do you know ...? A year is exactly 365.242199 days long, i.e. 365 days, five hours, 48 minutes and 46 seconds.

In England the New Year hasn't always begun on January 1st. Halloween was the Druids' New Year's Eve festival, so what is now our November 1st would have been their New Year. The Anglo Saxons then fixed the beginning of the year to coincide approximately with the sun's rebirth on around December 25th. Then most of Europe switched their New Year to the beginning of spring. So, for many years, March 25th was New Year's Day.

In fact most of Europe had been following the Julian calendar, which had been designed under the instructions of the Roman emperor Julius Caesar. But this calendar was too long by over 11 minutes a year, and after a number of centuries this amounted to 10 days. So in the 16th century Pope Gregory the 13th had a new calendar designed which revised the concept of leap years and set the beginning of the year to January 1st. Most of Europe then adopted this new calendar in around 1582, even though it meant cancelling 10 days.

The Scots changed to the Gregorian calendar in 1600, as it was obvious that any trading with other countries would be chaotic if they kept to the old Julian calendar. But the English held out until 1752 since they resented a Catholic pope telling them what to do. The Russians waited till 1918, and the Greeks till 1923. Eastern Orthodox churches and the Ethiopians still use the Julian calendar, which is why they celebrate Christmas and Easter approximately two weeks later than other Christians.

While most countries of the world have adopted the western Gregorian calendar for commercial purposes, some have still retained their old calendars for religious uses. Let's imagine that in the West we are in the year 2000. The Hindu calendar is then in the year 2056. The Muslim calendar is based on lunar years and begins in 622, the year when the Muslim prophet travelled from Mecca to Medina, so that our 2000 is their 1421. The Jewish system is based on the year the world was created, which was 3761 years before the beginning of the Christian era. Their year lasts from 354 to 385 days, thus they are in the year 5771.

2 Resolutions

1 Did you make any resolutions last year? What were they? Did you keep them?
2 What do you regret (not) having done last year?
3 What were the best/worst things that happened to you last year?
4 What three important things are going to happen to you in the coming year?
5 Is it important to make resolutions, and to have aims and ambitions in your life?

3 Which New Year?

1 Look at this calendar for October, 1582. What do you notice?

1582		OCTOBER				1582
M	T	W	T	F	S	S
1	2	3	4	15	16	17
18	19	20	21	22	23	24
25	26	27	28	29	30	31

2 New Year hasn't always begun on January 1. Complete the table.

New Year's Day	
Modern New Year	January 1
Druid New Year	
Anglo-Saxon New Year	
New Year in the Middle Ages	

3 In which year did the following countries change over to the Gregorian calendar?

Catholic Europe	1582
England	_____
Greece	_____
Russia	_____
Scotland	_____

4 Do you know exactly how long a year is? How many days, hours, etc?

DAY 2 Martin Luther King Jr's Birthday

Date	January 15
Level	intermediate
Age	all ages, especially teenagers
Time	Ex 1 15 minutes
	Ex 2 15 minutes
Advice	Political: some students may have problems talking about racism.
Vocabulary	seats, drinking fountains, non-violence, boycott, car pool, segregation, march, demonstrations, arrest, speech, dream, racism

1 Martin Luther King Jr's life

- Brainstorm to see what students know about MLK, the American human rights activist. What do they know about other similar leaders, e.g. Gandhi, Nelson Mandela? What were the differences between them?

- Hand out the photocopies and focus students' attention on the photos – in groups students try to work out what is happening and in what order the pictures should be (as preparation for the listening).

Listening 1

- Ask students to put the six pictures in order on the basis of what they hear in the listening passage.

 The correct order is 3 4 2 1 5 6.

Martin Luther King junior was born on 15 January 1929 in Atlanta, Georgia. He was a precocious child and was often top of his class. One day while on the bus to school, some white passengers got on. There were no seats free and the driver forced Martin and his friends to give up their seats. 'I don't think I have ever been so deeply angry in my life,' King later recalled. At that time there were not only separate bus seats for blacks and whites, but also separate drinking fountains, bathrooms and seats in restaurants.

While King was studying theology at university, he was impressed by the teachings of Mahatma Gandhi. King was convinced that the only way to fight against injustice was non-violence and non-resistance. Just before receiving his degree he became a pastor, like his father, of a Baptist church in Alabama.

In 1955 an African-American woman was arrested for refusing to give up her bus seat to a white person. King organised a year-long boycott of the buses and formed a car pool of 300 cars to take black people to work. Soon King was imprisoned for conspiracy to boycott a business. Some months later the Supreme Court of the United States freed King – his formula of passive resistance had won.

After this incident King travelled and delivered speeches demanding equal treatment for all peoples of the United States. King founded a movement which secured black people's right to vote, and ended the segregation of public facilities in the South. He went on to organise the massive march on Washington, where he gave his famous 'I have a dream' speech on August 28, 1963. The following year King became the youngest person to win the Nobel Peace Prize.

Early in 1968, King began to plan a multi-racial poor people's march on Washington to demand an end to all discrimination. But he was assassinated in Memphis, Tennessee on 4 April 1968, perhaps by the paid agent of FBI conspirators or white extremists. Riots and demonstrations in 125 cities protested against his killing – 46 people died and over 20,000 were arrested.

- For more advanced students, after the picture ordering activity, dictate the following questions, or display them on an OHP, and ask students to write a summary which includes answers to the questions:

1 Where and when was MLK born?
2 What happened to MLK at school?
3 What job did his father do?
4 What did MLK study at university?
5 What do you think a car pool is?
6 Why was MLK sent to prison?
7 Where and in which year did he give his 'I have a dream' speech?
8 What was particular about him winning the Nobel Peace Prize?
9 When was he assassinated and by whom?
10 How many people died and were arrested in the riots which followed his killing?

- Lower level students could just answer the questions.

Song

- King's birthday was made a federal holiday in 1983 after consistent campaigning by, among others, Stevie Wonder, who dedicated a song to MLK, *Happy Birthday* on his CD *Master Blaster*.

Follow-up

- Students discuss which political figure in their country (past or present) they think should be honoured with a public holiday or at least with a song!

2 I have a dream

- In pairs, students read the extract from MLK's speech, and fill in any of the gaps they feel sure of with one or more words. They should then choose appropriate words from the box to fill in any remaining gaps. Play **Listening 2** for students to check their answers.

1 friends   **2** difficulties   **3** dream   **4** American   **5** day
6 meaning   **7** created equal   **8** red hills   **9** together
10 injustice   **11** freedom   **12** four children
13 color of their skin   **14** hands

DAY 2 Martin Luther King Jr's Birthday

1 Martin Luther King Jr's life

2 I have a dream

I say to you today, my ———————— [1], so even though we face the ———————— [2] of today and tomorrow, I still have a ———————— [3].
It is a dream deeply rooted in the ———————— [4] dream.

I have a dream that one ———————— [5] this nation will rise up and live out the true ———————— [6] of its creed: "We hold these truths to be self-evident: that all men are ———————— [7]."

I have a dream that one day on the ———————— [8] of Georgia, the sons of former slaves and the sons of former slaveowners will be able to sit down ———————— [9] at the table of brotherhood.

I have a dream that one day even the state of Mississippi, a state, sweltering with the heat of ———————— [10], sweltering with the heat of oppression, will be transformed into an oasis of ———————— [11] and justice.

I have a dream that my ———————— [12] will one day live in a nation where they will not be judged by the ———————— [13] but by the content of their character. I have a dream today.

I have a dream that one day down in Alabama, with its vicious racists, with its governor having his lips dripping with the words of interposition and nullification, one day right down in Alabama little black boys and black girls will be able to join ———————— [14] with little white boys and white girls as sisters and brothers. I have a dream today.

American	dream	injustice
color of their skin	four children	meaning
together	freedom	created equal
day	friends	red hills
difficulties	hands	

DAY 3 Valentine's Day

Date	February 14
Level	Exs 1 and 2 lower intermediate
	Exs 3 and 4 intermediate
Age	teenagers
Time	Ex 1 10 minutes
	Ex 2 10 minutes
	Ex 3 10 minutes
	Ex 4 10 minutes
	Ex 5 20 minutes
Advice	Ex 3 discusses relationships with the opposite sex.
Vocabulary	card, celebrate, kids, present, love poems/messages, fancy someone, fall in love, blind date, opposite sex

(Saint) Valentine's Day is a lovers' day and is celebrated on 14 February, and not just in the West – the Japanese, too, go in for it in a big way. In the US, teachers get more Valentine cards than anyone else, followed by children, mothers, wives, and finally sweethearts! Some South and Central American countries also have a Friends' Day, hence the 'ideal friend' exercise in this unit, which means that those students who feel uneasy talking about love can at least talk about friendship.

1 Who was St Valentine?

- Before handing out photocopies ask students to tell you what, if anything, they know about St Valentine.
- Hand out photocopies and ask students to look at the illustrations and imagine what the stories behind them might be. Then proceed to the listening activity.

Listening 1

- Students hear three stories of the possible origins of St Valentine, which are illustrated on the page. Their task is to match the stories with the pictures and then decide which is true. NB There is one extra picture.

🔑 **1** b   **2** c   **3** a

No one really knows the true origin of St Valentine's Day. Until 1969 February 14 was a designated saint's day in the Roman Catholic calendar. The Claudius referred to in the listening was Claudius II who ruled from 268–270 AD.

1 On February 14th our ancestors believed that birds began to choose their partners and to mate on this day. In fact some people still believe that the first bird you see on this day will foretell who your future husband is going to be.

2 Valentine was a Roman priest who was jailed in the third century by the Emperor Claudius for marrying young couples. Claudius had made a law against this because he thought that soldiers who were single were better fighters than married ones. While he was in jail, Valentine fell in love with the jailer's blind daughter. He managed to restore her sight and before his execution he left her a message which simply said: From your Valentine.

3 February 15th was the date of the Roman love festival of Lupercalia. On this day young Romans gave each other presents. Another custom was for the names of young men and women to be shaken in a box and then drawn like a lottery to make love couples.

2 How do you celebrate Valentine's Day?

- Students read the texts and decide which one is most similar to the way they celebrate Valentine's Day. What sort of cards do they send? Romantic or humorous?

3 Valentine messages

- Give students time to read the messages, then ask them to draw or write their own cards or Valentine messages, such as you might find in a personal column of a newspaper.

Follow-up

- On a less romantic note, some third-world countries, particularly in Africa, have turned over grain-producing fields (some for home consumption) to cultivate flowers for western occasions such as Valentine's Day. You might like to ask students to discuss what they think about this.

DAY 3 Valentine's Day

1 Who was St Valentine?

a

b

c

d

2 How do you celebrate Valentine's Day?

a *When you're young you send a card to a girl you like. But you don't sign your name so they don't know who it's from. And kids sometimes send cards to their parents.*

(Niall O'Cuillin, Republic of Ireland)

b *In Norway we don't have Valentine's Day, but I think it's a really good idea.*

(Gunn-Marit Øygarden, Norway)

c *Here in Indonesia teenagers have just begun celebrating Valentine's Day – they love it!*

(Dewi Chandrasa, Indonesia)

d *My mother told me that they didn't have Valentine's Day when she was young, so it must be quite a recent thing.*

(Anna Maria Filep, Hungary)

e *In Japan it's so popular that we have two days. On February 14 girls give chocolates to boys, and young ladies give their boss an 'obligation' present. Then on March 14, which is called 'White Day', boys have to express their love to girls. I think this was all invented by the chocolate companies.*

(Midori Yamamoto, Japan)

f *My daughter sends a card to her pet, like a lot of American pet owners. I've read that over a billion Valentine cards are sent every year in the States, and most of them are to teachers like me.*

(Kim Hancock, USA)

g *In Denmark we send flowers, poems and love messages which contain a series of dots, one dot for each letter of your name. If the person you send the message to guesses that you have sent it, then you have to give them an egg at Easter. But if they don't get your name, they have to pay a forfeit.*

(Lina Thorgaard, Denmark)

3 Valentine messages

SARAH
Who said love hurts?
They are not wrong.
ALAN

The love bulbs planted last autumn will flower with summer's dawn and last forever.

George
Roses are red, violets are blue,
I can't bear to spend my life without you.
Sally

xxx PAULA xxx
Someone somewhere adores you.
Can you guess who?

To D.C.B.
Delightful, charming and beautiful too,
These words express my love for you.
From F.C.J.

P.F.C.
Memory can be faulty, but memories never fade.
Malcolm

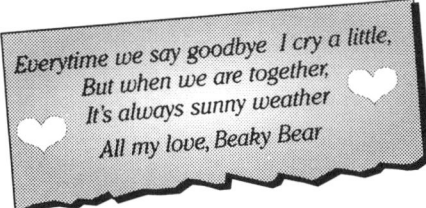
Everytime we say goodbye I cry a little,
But when we are together,
It's always sunny weather
All my love, Beaky Bear

H.T.
I love you with all my heart.
It's such a shame we had to part.
The time has come to sort things through.
Make up your mind – it's up to you.
J.F.F.

susie K
My love is here to stay.
Please be my
valentine today.
Mike S.

4 How romantic are you?

- Decide whether this exercise is suitable for your students. If not, do exercise 5 instead. Hand out photocopies.
- Students do the quiz, and then compare and discuss their answers.
- Alternatively, students can invent their own quiz or at least add some questions. For cultural and taboo problems I didn't write questions such as:
- Who would you most like to spend the night with?
- What is the best way to find a partner?
- Which film would you most like to watch with your partner?
- Which part of your partner's body do you find most attractive?
   But there's no reason why with the right students you couldn't think up some questions on these lines.

1b Choosing the right flowers and the right number (odd numbers for the living, even numbers for the dead) is of paramount importance in many countries – find out traditions in your students' countries.

3c Greta Garbo once said: 'Love is a romantic designation for a most ordinary biological – or shall we say, chemical? – process. A lot of nonsense is talked and written about it.' Scientists have proved that it is indeed a chemical process; the feelings of euphoria and elation (that begin to wane after two or three years) are caused by phenylethylamine, dopamine and norepinephrine. After the attraction phase is over, attachment takes over and larger amounts of endorphins (chemically similar to morphine) flow into the brain, leaving lovers with a sense of security, peace and calm. There is also the famous 'cuddle chemical' oxytocin which stimulates sensations during lovemaking and produces feelings of relaxed satisfaction and attachment.

Films

- Ask students to bring in a video with their favourite love/romantic scene (i.e. dialogue with a minimum of physical contact and certainly no sex!). Having watched the scene, students could then act it out.

Songs

- Ask students to bring in a recording of their favourite English language love song. They could listen and write down any words that they can decipher and then sing it out loud!

5 Friends' Day

- Tell students that in Argentina (and other Central and South American countries) they celebrate Friends' Day. Young Argentineans send each other presents (flowers, books), write each other letters saying why that person is their best friend, and at school elect the most popular person in the class. Ask students if they would like to introduce a similar day.
- Students then do the quiz individually before comparing their answers with their partner.
- Ask for feedback on whether they would have answered differently if the questions had regarded their ideal partner rather than their ideal friend.

Listening 2

- Students listen to two girls (who incidentally are best friends in real life, authentic recording) talking about their ideal friend. Students should identify what ideas they have in common. They can then discuss whether they agree with the two girls.

The ideas they have in common are: a friend is someone you can trust and someone you can tell secrets to.

1 I think my ideal friend would be someone you can trust, someone who you can tell your secrets to, and someone who of course would keep the secrets, someone who'll be honest with you, and who you can just be yourself around, you don't have to feel like you have to be somebody else and someone that you like get along with and that you have fun with. That's just an ideal friend to me.

2 An ideal friend to me it wouldn't matter if it was a boy or a girl, or anything. As long as I could trust them, and tell my secrets, and if they were understanding, and then ... I'd have to pull my part in being in having a friendship. He or she would have to understand me, and you know, try to help me with my problems.

4

How romantic are you?

 1 *What does Valentine's Day mean to you?*
- *a* It's the day when you find out who really fancies you.
- *b* It's a good excuse for buying your partner flowers or chocolates.
- *c* It's just a commercial event.

 2 *What do you do with your old Valentine cards and presents?*
- *a* I keep them forever.
- *b* I've kept one or two special ones.
- *c* I recycle them.

 3 *Which group of sentences is most true?*
- *a* I fall in love easily. I've had my heart broken many times. I feel lost if I'm not in a relationship.
- *b* I like flirting. I don't want a serious relationship. Love is important, but not the most important thing in my life.
- *c* I have more friends of my own sex than the opposite sex. Love is a chemical process and that's all.

4 *What is the most important element of a long-lasting relationship?*
- *a* Love.
- *b* Friendship.
- *c* Economic security.

Score Give yourself two points for every **a**, one for every **b**, and none for a **c**.

6–8 You are an incurable romantic. But be careful, love hurts too.

3–5 You are romantic and realistic at the same time. You always come out of a relationship on top.

0–2 Love for you is a business. You are ruled totally by your head, never by your heart. Ironically, you are more likely to have a long-lasting relationship than people who scored higher than you in the test.

5

 My ideal friend... FRIENDS' DAY

1
- **a** is the same age as me.
- **b** is a little younger.
- **c** is a little older.

2
- **a** is the same sex as me.
- **b** is the opposite sex.

3
- **a** is as good looking as me.
- **b** is not as good looking as me.
- **c** is better looking than me.
- **d** Looks are irrelevant.

4
- **a** is as intelligent as me.
- **b** is not as intelligent as me.
- **c** is more intelligent than me.
- **d** Intelligence is irrelevant.

5
- **a** never hides anything from me.
- **b** keeps the truth from me if he/she knows it will hurt me.

6
- **a** has basically the same views of life as me.
- **b** has different views.

7
- **a** has similar interests to me.
- **b** has different interests.

8 *Which of the following statements do you agree with?*
- **a** The older you are, the more difficult it is to make friends.
- **b** You should be more loyal to your friends than to your lovers.
- **c** You shouldn't believe your friends when they ask you to be honest with them.
- **d** Friendships between females are stronger than friendships between males.
- **e** You can't truly be friends with someone of the opposite sex.

DAY 4 Carnival

Date	February, varies
Level	intermediate
Age	all ages
Time	Ex 1 20 minutes
	Ex 2 10 minutes
Vocabulary	carnival, costumes, float, fan, procession, gods, celebration, Lent, Epiphany, pagan, rite, fasting, festival, mask, priest, practical joke, fancy dress ball

This could be done in conjunction with Day 5: Fasting.

In Christian countries Carnival usually coincides with Shrovetide, the four days before the beginning of Lent, a time of fasting. Carnivals, therefore, are principally held in February, although this varies from nation to nation, and also from region to region. The origins of Carnival are explained on the cassette.

1 Carnival quiz

- Hand out photocopies and ask students to do the quiz in groups before listening to the cassette, which will give them the answers to questions 3–7.

  (Question 1: Rio, New Orleans, Venice, etc.)

Listening

- Students hear an extract from a radio talk show about Carnivals. They should listen and check their answers to questions 3–7.

 3 'Taking away the meat' from *carne levamen* (Latin).
  4 Fat Tuesday. People fatten up before fasting.
  6 Portugal, France.
  7 Yes.

> A So, what does 'Carnival' actually mean?
> B Well, the period after Carnival is Lent, and you weren't supposed to eat meat during Lent, so the word 'Carnival' actually comes from the Latin *carne levamen*, meaning 'taking away the meat'.
> A Right.
> B Carnival time traditionally begins after Epiphany, or Twelfth Night, and leads up to Mardi Gras, which literally means Fat Tuesday, and was a time when everyone ate as much food as they could before fasting in Lent.
> A So when did it all begin?
> B Probably with the Romans and Greeks. It was really part of their spring festivals, and they wore masks and ...

> A But it's actually part of the Catholic calendar, isn't it?
> B Well, it is and it isn't. Like most Christian festivities it was based on pagan rites, but the church didn't manage to quash the fun part. Just as the Greeks and Romans played jokes on each other at this time of year, later so did the people of many European countries, especially Italy, France, Spain and Portugal.
> A And when the Portuguese and French settled in the New World, did they take their traditions with them?
> B Yes, in fact when the Portuguese landed in Brazil they brought with them the *entrudo*, which was a kind of practical joke, and people used to throw water and flour at each other. And in later periods the African slaves were allowed to join in the fun too.
> A But didn't things get out of hand?
> B Well, yes, they did, and it's interesting because exactly the same things were going on up in New Orleans in Louisiana, which of course was under French rule. The slaves there as well were going around disguised with masks. And the music and dance in both places still today have strong African influences.
> A I suppose in New Orleans, Rio de Janeiro and Venice people have always had great fun outdoors, with the dancing, parades and what have you ...

2 Carnival in Brazil

- Students read the text for interest.

Follow-up

- In groups students can do one of the following tasks: i) plan a fancy dress party ii) design a carnival float. Both activities require lots of suggestions to be made.
- For i) they need to decide on a theme, when and where to hold the party, who to invite, where to get the costumes from, etc. They also need to design the invitations.
- For ii) they need to decide on a theme: will it be political, something to do with a famous singer or actor, a scene from history, etc? They also need to work out the technicalities of making and pulling the float, and who will go on it, etc. Their first task should thus be to draw up a list of these factors and then discuss them.
- Alternatively, in groups students could create a collage to depict how they would like their float to look. Then you could elect a panel of judges to decide which is the best collage.

DAY 4 Carnival

1 Carnival quiz

1 Name three towns famous for their carnivals.

2 Which of the following activities do you like most about Carnival time:

  a playing jokes on other people
  b organising and going to parties
  c preparing special foods
  d making and wearing masks and costumes
  e dancing in the streets
  f making floats
  g watching parades
  h burning floats and effigies

3 What is the origin of the word 'carnival'?

4 What does 'Mardi Gras' mean? Why is it so called?

5 Did Carnival begin as a Christian festival?

6 Which European countries took the Carnival to Brazil and New Orleans (US)?

7 Are there African influences in the Carnival both in Brazil and New Orleans (US)?

2

Carnival in Brazil

For many residents of São Paulo and Rio de Janeiro, especially the poor, 'Carnaval' is the highlight of their year. Literally within days of the end of one carnival the Escolas de Samba (samba schools) begin preparing their dances for the next year.

The carnival lasts for the five days up to and including Terça-Feira (Shrove/Fat Tuesday) and comes at the end of the summer holidays in Brazil. It is not just a time for fun, it is also a highly competitive occasion on which groups of between 1 500 and 4 000 people compete to see who can dance best and create the most original costumes and carros alegoricos (floats). This competition is organised like a football league, with the samba schools moving up and down grupos (divisions) depending on how well they dance in their categories. And like the supporters at a football match, there are fans at the carnival who scream for their escola.

Every year each school chooses a particular theme for their carnival procession. This theme generally relates to a historical event or personality. If the theme is, for example, some famous person, the words to the songs recount their life story. If this person is still alive, like the famous Brazilian writer Jorge Amado or the actress Dercy Gonçalves, then they may take part in the carnival themselves.

Some schools dedicate their carnival to gods from Afro-Brazilian religions. In fact, from the 16th to the 19th century, African slaves worked for the Portuguese in the plantations. So today carnivals in Brazil are a mixture of native, African and European cultures. After all the celebrations are over, many members of the samba schools go on world tours to raise money for next year's carnival.

◀ ◀ ◀ ◀ ◀ ◀ ◀ ◀ ◀ ◀ ◀ ◀ ◀ ◀ ◀

DAY 5 Fasting

Date	varies
Level	upper intermediate
Age	mature teenagers and adults
Time	Ex 1 10 minutes
	Ex 2 10 minutes
	Ex 3 15 minutes
Grammar	modals of permission and obligation: *can, be allowed to, have to*
Vocabulary	fasting, wilderness, purify, sunset, sunrise, worship, spiritual, restriction, forbid, give up, Lent, Jew, Orthodox, starve

This lesson can be done after Day 4: Carnival. The Carnival period in Christian countries usually precedes the period of fasting known as Lent.

Early Christians, particularly monks, had a hard time as far as food was concerned. On the 200 fast days in the year (Wednesdays, Fridays, Saturdays and the period of Lent) they could only have dried biscuits dunked in broth plus a little bread. The idea was to calm the appetite for food, which in turn would suppress sexual hunger too. Later, in the sixth century, they were allowed two meals a day, mainly consisting of vegetables. To satisfy their hunger the monks rustled up some intriguing recipes. Things got better when they were allowed to eat fish, and the definition of what was not meat became conveniently flexible, so that they allowed themselves to eat the fully developed foetus of a rabbit (apparently a great delicacy); frogs became classified as fish, as were beavers, because they use their tails to swim!

1 Lent

- Ask students if they fast, when, how often and why.
- Before you give out photocopies, fold each one over so that students cannot see the Ramadan texts yet.
- Hand out the photocopies and tell students not to look at the folded over text yet.
- Students read the Lent text for interest and then decide three things they are going to give up for Lent (or that they want to give up anyway). They discuss with a partner why they want to give them up, and which ones they are most/least likely to succeed with.

Follow-up

- One of the original aims of Christian fasting, and going without meat, was to bring the rich people closer to the poor. Get students to think of more modern methods of redressing the balance, e.g. sleeping on the streets with the homeless.

2 Yom Kippur

- Students read the texts and then, in combination with the text in Exercise 1, compare their fasting habits.

3 Ramadan

- Before students look at this section, brainstorm with them what they know about Ramadan and what Muslims can and cannot do during this period. Then ask them to fold open their page and read the texts to see how much corresponds with what they said.

Listening

- Students hear a Muslim woman from Pakistan discussing Ramadan. As they listen, they should match points (a–f) on their page with the listening extracts. N.B. One point is mentioned twice, and one not at all. Consider not playing the second part of extract 6 if you think your students might be embarrassed.

 1 d   **2** a   **3** e   **4** c   **5** f   **6** a (Point b is not mentioned.)

1 There's something called the *Zakat* that you have to pay, which is 2.5% of your cash savings, which goes away as charity, that you have to pay in the month of Ramadan, you ... it's your savings plus things like jewellery, gold, diamonds or whatever you have, you have to pay 2.5% of that too and give give it away to charity.

2 Oh right Eid is a celebration of the completion of the Qu'ran. The full of revelation of the Qu'ran. And we say that during the month of Ramadan, the Qu'ran was revealed to the prophet Mohammed and Eid is basically a celebration of the fact that we've got our holy book now.

3 And basically the Islamic calendar is according to the lunar calendar, which means that it's that for example, Eid is ten days before every year, so it can fall any time of the year in your life. And so of course you work. I mean you can't sort of put school curriculum in you know in accordance with Ramadan for example or Eid because there is no such thing as Ramadan falling during the summer so you know that you're on holiday and you can fast and there are no problems, it's not like that.

4 It is sort of like a way of purifying your body because you're purifying your mind as well as, you know, your spiritual state, your relationship with your religion, you're it's just you're starting all over again.

5 We end the fast at about just after sunset. Just after sunset because because um it's not to be confused with the fact it's not to be confused with the sun worshippers who would start something from the rise, you know from the beginning from when the sun rose and end something when the sun would go down.

6 What you can't do is basically you can't eat. You can't eat at all. You can't drink water, you can't drink anything. // And you can't have sexual intercourse, and well any kind of sexual activity is prohibited during that time because you're it's a completely spiritual activity, you're only doing it, it's just between you and God.

DAY 5 Fasting

1

Lent Fasting means not eating food, in fact 'breakfast' literally means 'breaking the fast', as it is the first food you have at the beginning of a day. Lent is a 40-day (not counting Sundays) fast for the Christian church, in imitation of Christ's fasting in the wilderness. For the Church of England there are three important things to do during Lent: prayer, almsgiving (giving money, food and clothes to the poor) and fasting. Originally, you could only have one meal a day on fast days (of which there were 200 a year), and you were allowed to eat only vegetables – no meat or animal products. Later, eggs, fish and shell fish became permissible. Today very few people observe this fast, though many Catholics still eat fish on a Friday and fast on Ash Wednesday (the first day of Lent) and Good Friday (the last Friday in Lent, before Easter Sunday).

The idea of the Lent fast survives in the tradition of Pancake Tuesday. This is the name given now to Shrove Tuesday, the day before the beginning of Lent. People used to make pancakes to use up all their eggs and fat, which they were forbidden to eat during Lent, and it is still traditional to eat pancakes on this day. There are a number of events on Shrove Tuesday associated with eggs and pancakes, such as egg and spoon races, pancake races, pancake tossing, etc. For most people the only element of fasting that remains is the custom of giving up things you enjoy for the period of Lent, such as eating chocolate.

2 Yom Kippur

a Jewish people fast before Yom Kippur (the Day of Atonement). It is a time for thinking about our lives. We believe that during this period you should do everything you can to put right things that you have done wrong. We do various things to help us concentrate better: women aren't allowed to wear make-up, you can't wear shoes with leather soles, and you're not supposed to feel comfortable, so we sit on low stools. No food is eaten. No liquid is drunk. No work is done. And all this helps you to think about people who are starving. In fact, the money we save by fasting we give to an agency that helps the hungry.

(Marc Ferster, Britain)

b In order to understand that we are all dependent on God's providence, we abstain from food and drink for a period of 25 hours, after which we in the West are fortunate enough to eat heartily, whereas two thirds of the world's population will experience 'fasting' every day of their lives.

(Douglas Charing, Five World Faiths, Cassell 1991)

3 Ramadan

a *Ramadan is the month when the Qu'ran was revealed to Prophet Mohammed. We fast, and pray in the Mosque. We can't drink or eat for 10 or 11 hours. At the end of Ramadan we celebrate Eid, and we send each other cards.*

(Dewi Chandrasa, Indonesia)

b *We fast for God. We fast to feel like poor people – to create a feeling of equality. It helps to give us a strong will power and to fight against bad habits. We give food to poor people.*

(Mohamed Aly Sow, Senegal)

c *We fast because in the Qu'ran it is written that you must fast. And we fast to purify our bodies.*

(Hanadi Shehab, Saudi Arabia)

d *We have something called Zakat, which is about 2.5% of our cash savings that Muslims give to charity, though sometimes we give cattle and crops instead.*

(Mohamed Khalil, Palestine)

e *Ramadan is not always at the same time of year because it is decided by the lunar calendar.*

(Muna Zunoon, Sudan)

f *We get up just before sunrise. This was originally done to distinguish the followers of Mohammed from the sun worshippers. Then we fast until just after sunset. The number of hours depends on where you live in the world, the number of hours of daylight.*

(Aouadi Nadjet, Algeria)

DAY 6 Women's Day

Date	March 8
Level	upper intermediate
Age	mature teenagers and adults
Time	Ex 1 20 minutes
	Ex 2 25 minutes
	Ex 3 15 minutes
Advice	Brings into question traditional gender roles.
Grammar	Ex 2 comparisons
Vocabulary	garment, textile, wages, equality, trampled, campaign, rally, socialist, suffrage, murder, death penalty, discriminate, suicide, homeless

The notes in the Key on the Students' Page omit a lot of political details about the origins of Women's Day, which are outlined here for those interested.

The women demonstrators from the 1857 protest then formed their own trade union, but did not continue with annual demonstrations on that date. Decades later an incipient socialist party emerged. That party established a Women's National Committee (WNC) which held demonstration days, including an annual National Women's Day – initially celebrated on the last Sunday in February.

The WNC leaders communicated frequently with overseas socialist women's organisations. Clara Zetkin of the German Social Democrats approved of the American socialist women and their annual Women's Day, and was successful in her own lobbying effort to get the Second International to declare an annual 'International Proletarian Women's Day'.

By 1913, International Women's Day was used by participants to protest against the impending world war.

In 1917, the celebration of International Women's Day by Petrograd women set in motion the revolution which toppled the 304-year-old Romanov dynasty. Their demonstration against wartime suffering and factory conditions produced such massive support, not only from the factory women but from housewives and women in the street, that it forced male revolutionaries to join in the movement too.

After the war, celebration of the holiday continued, as it was adopted by non-socialist feminists as well as socialists. Both women's organisations and the Left promoted it, as did the trade union movement. 8 March was an official holiday in socialist countries such as the Soviet Union and China, but, like May Day, it became something of a cynical manipulation of a popular symbol.

1 Women, work, and politics

- Before you hand out photocopies, you may want to cut off the key at the bottom of the page so that you can hand it out separately after the students have done the quiz.
- Ask students to look at the photos and decide which women they admire most, who has achieved the most, etc. Who would they most like to have been?

- Ask students to write down who they think are/have been the three most important or famous women in the history of their country or of the world. In groups they compare their answers.
- Ask students if they have a Women's Day in their country and when and how it is celebrated. Are the celebrations purely political? Or is it simply a time when women get together, go out for a meal, give each other flowers (or the men give them flowers) and children give their female teachers sweets, flowers and other gifts?
- Students now do the quiz. The answers to questions 1, 2, 4 and 5 are in the key at the bottom of the Students' Page. For the answer to question 3, I have listed here the dates that refer to countries you are most likely to have students from. Sources differ surprisingly as to the exact date of women's suffrage in some countries – apologies for any inaccuracies and also if your country is not listed.

1893	New Zealand	1902	Australia
1906	Finland	1913	Norway
1915	Denmark	1917	Russia
1918	Canada	1918	UK
1919	Austria	1919	Czechoslovakia
1919	Germany	1919	Netherlands
1919	Poland	1920	Belgium
1920	USA	1921	India
1921	Sweden	1932	Thailand
1934	Turkey	1936	Costa Rica
1937	Philippines	1940	Cuba
1942	Spain	1942	Venezuela
1944	Mongolia	1945	Japan
1945	Italy	1945	Portugal
1945	Hungary	1945	Guatemala
1946	Brazil	1946	Ecuador
1946	France	1946	Romania
1947	Argentina	1947	China
1948	Israel	1948	Korea
1949	Chile	1949	Indonesia
1949	Syria	1952	Lebanon
1956	Egypt	1957	Colombia
1963	Iran	1980	Iraq

- Use the quiz as a stimulus to get students thinking about the position of women today (at work, in politics, at home), focusing on significant milestones in women's history.
- As a more light-hearted alternative, get students to imagine that a Martian has just landed. In groups, their task is to define what the main differences are between men and women. Groups can then compare their ideas and vote on which group came up with the funniest and most original definitions, or the most perceptive and insightful ones.

DAY 6 Women's Day

1 Women, work and politics

Eva Peron

Margaret Thatcher

Madonna

Naomi Campbell

Mother Theresa

Princess Diana

Quiz

1 *The origin of Women's Day goes back to*
  a the French Revolution.
  b around 150 years ago in the USA.
  c the Women's Liberation movement in the 1960s.

2 *The first country where women got the vote was*
  a Australia. **b** Finland. **c** New Zealand.

3 *Women in your country got the vote*
  a before 1914.
  b between 1915 and 1939.
  c between 1940 and 1960.
  d after 1960.

4 *Women in the world do how much of the world's work?*
  a 10% **b** 33% **c** 66%

5 *The average woman earns what percentage of the average man's salary for doing the same job?*
  a 100% **b** 80% **c** 60%

Key

1 b **2** c **3** Ask your teacher. **4** c **5** b

On 8 March 1857 women garment and textile workers demonstrated on the Lower East Side of New York City. They demanded equality for women at work: they were angry about low wages and a twelve-hour working day. The march was dispersed by the police. Some women were arrested, others were trampled in the confusion.

On 8 March 1908 Women's Day was commemorated for the first time by thousands of women clothing workers from the same New York district. There was a street demonstration demanding the right to vote, shorter working hours, legislation against child labour, and better working conditions.

On 8 March 1911 the first international celebrations of Women's Day were held: more than one million women and men attended rallies in Austria, Denmark, Germany and Switzerland, demanding the right to vote and hold office, plus the right to work, to vocational training, and an end to discrimination on the job.

New Zealand was the first country to give women the vote, in 1893, followed by Australia in 1902 and Finland in 1906.

2 Whose liberation?

- Before you hand out photocopies, either cut off the key at the bottom of the page or fold it up so that students are not tempted to try to read the answers before they do Exercise 2.

- In groups students decide which sex has a better position in society, and then whether the statements on their page are true or false (all US statistics).

- Students then find the mixed up answers in the key at the bottom of the page and have to match the answer with the question.

- As whole class, hypothesise on the reasons behind the statistics.

All the statements are false: **a** 3 **b** 5 **c** 4 **d** 7 **e** 2 **f** 6 **g** 1

Listening

- Four adults discuss the pros and cons of Women's and Men's Day. Ask students to listen and answer these questions:

1 What reasons do the women give for there not being a Men's Day?

2 Do either of the women think Men's Day would be a good idea? If so, why? If not, why not?

3 What is the aim of Women's Day according to one of the female speakers?

1 Men have the other 364 days; men haven't felt the need for their own day.

2 Yes. Men lost power to feminism, need to regain ground.

3 It gives an opportunity to talk about women's rights and women in other countries.

A But now we're in, we're living in an age where sexual equality is is is the thing. And there's no need for it. I mean if that's the case why don't we have a Men's Day?

B Because ... you don't have a Men's Day because you get the other 364. [Oooh!]

C Well, actually I mean why don't you have a Men's Day? Obviously men haven't felt the need for one, in the same way that women have.

A You think it's still as valid to have a Woman's Day?

C I think it would be valid to have both actually. I think it's always a good idea to ...

A So where do you stand on women's lib then, if that's the case?

C Well, I think that a lot's changed over the last 20 years, and in fact I feel rather sorry for men these days, because I think the whole women's lib thing has become so strong, men have actually lost a lot of their sort of powers. And I think they need to come back now. Because feminism has, you know, become so overpowering.

D So what do you do? Do you send each other cards?

B Well, I don't actually think that Women's Day necessarily has anything to do with women's lib or feminism. [Right] No, not at all. I think it's just an acknowledgement of women and I think it came about at a time when women didn't have many rights and it makes you think about these kinds of questions and how many countries there still are in the world where women don't have rights.

C Is it celebrated in India?

B As far as I know it isn't, but there are states in India which are communist and I know it was taken up by the communist countries, so therefore I would think they would know about it. There are many countries that are much further ahead than we are here in England, let's face it.

C And there are also many countries who still regard women as a lower lower race.

---

3 F, N or M?

- Dictate some or all of the words in the box below.

father, sister, son, Mr, baby, person, husband, heir, doctor, secretary, president, housewife, footballer, actress, soldier, dancer, policeman, manager, lion, cow, cook, aunt, professor, waiter, lady, bride, sales assistant, cousin, niece, queen, cleaner, scout, hero, nurse, thief, host, tramp, doll, pedestrian, priest, victim, monk, gypsy, widow, duchess, spinster.

- As you dictate the words, students write them into an appropriate place in the diagram: exclusively female words (sister, housewife) on the left (F), neutral words (baby, doctor) in the middle (N), and exclusively male words (father, husband) on the right (M).

- Students then compare their diagrams, particularly looking at the middle area, i.e. words like 'doctor' which refer to both sexes. Should priests always be male? This should lead on to a discussion on gender roles and political correctness.

- As a whole-class activity, get feedback from students. Highlight i) 'real' mistakes, e.g. classifying 'cousin' as a masculine, when it is actually a gender-free word and ii) mistakes of 'political correctness', e.g. putting 'cleaner' as feminine when again it is gender free.

- Now ask students to decide on the male equivalents of the female words and vice versa (Mr vs Ms vs Mrs or Miss). Also ask them to find unisex equivalents of words like policeman (police officer), etc.

Follow-up

- Divide the class into male and female groups. The females write down the five worst things about a man, and the males do the same about a woman.

- Rearrange them into small groups containing both sexes and let them battle it out!

2 Whose liberation?

True or false?

a Women have always lived about 10 years longer than men.
b Women work longer hours than men (including housework, shopping, etc.).
c Far more women are victims of violence than men.
d There are as many homeless women as there are homeless men.
e Proportionally as many female as male murderers receive the death penalty.
f Only women are discriminated against at work.
g A wife whose husband dies is much more likely to commit suicide than a husband whose wife dies.

3 F, N or M?

Key to 2 Whose liberation?

1 A husband whose wife dies is about 10 times more likely to commit suicide than a wife whose husband dies.

2 A man convicted of murder is 20 times more likely than a woman convicted of murder to receive the death penalty.

3 In 1920, women in the USA lived one year longer than men. Today women live seven years longer. Men die earlier than women from all 15 of the leading causes of death.

4 Men are twice as likely to be victims of violent crimes, and three times more likely to be murdered.

5 The average man works 61 hours per week including doing yardwork, repairs, and painting; women do 56 hours.

6 The US Supreme Court ruled in 1987 that in job areas dominated by men, less qualified women could be hired. It did not allow less qualified men to be hired in areas dominated by women.

7 85% of the homeless are men.

DAY 7 Mother's Day

Date	varies
	UK: 4th Sunday in Lent
	US: 2nd Sunday in May
Level	Ex 1 lower/upper intermediate
	Ex 2 upper intermediate
Age	all ages
Time	Ex 1 15 minutes
	Ex 2 15 minutes
Vocabulary	rip off, stationery department, playgroup, surrogacy, artificial insemination, prolific, maternal instinct

See page 106 for information about the origins of Mother's Day.

1 Mummy, mom, mama

- Before handing out photocopies, ask students to write down some statements that they associate with their mother and with their father. For example, *I look like him/her, I have more in common with him/her, he/she was always stricter with me. I have learnt more from her/him.* In pairs, students read out their lists and their partner has to guess which parent the statements refer to. This should lead onto a discussion of the roles of parents.

- Hand out photocopies. Let students look at the children's pictures and comments for interest. Students now mark the statements in the exercise true or false in accordance with their relationship with their mothers. They then discuss their answers.

Listening 1 (for higher levels only)

- Students hear some British adults discussing Mother's Day. Pre-teach 'kids' and dictate the following questions for students to answer.
1 How many speakers have children?
2 What things do people buy their mothers in Britain?
3 Does the man's mother like Mother's Day?
4 What is the husband's role on Mother's Day?
5 What do children do for their mothers?

 1 One.
   2 Cards and flowers and maybe a little present.
   3 No.
   4 He has to buy a card for the child to give their mother.
   5 Make things at school.

> **A** Well, you know, years ago I did what every kid did. I went out and got ripped off by the stationery department buying very expensive cards, and the florist, buying dead flowers. But I'm actually a very new mum myself and I like it [incomprehensible]

> **B** If I was a mum, which I'm not yet, [no, no] but if I was a mum, I ... I would like it as well. My mum is so strange about hol... those kind of celebrations, she doesn't like, you know mothers, but she does she doesn't like them, she doesn't encourage sort of, she doesn't expect anything, she doesn't really want to ...

> **C** Now you see but she might if she ... [I'm sure] Now you see my mother says 'I've got no time for it at all, it's American rubbish,' and then, but she'd be furious if there wasn't a card, if there wasn't the flowers, there wasn't the little present, you know, so that's different, it's a sort of double standard.

> **A** But it is nice and it's also nice for the husbands just for a minute to have to go out and buy the card for the child to give the mum to say 'thank you'.

> **C** I hadn't thought of it like that, because I haven't got any kids, but you know ...

> **A** Well, it is. And that's what I'm saying as a new mum. I mean before I was terribly cynical about it, and it is a rip-off, all of these things [yes, yes] are actually kind of rip-offs and it would be much nicer, which is also a thing that my little girl does, she makes things at playgroup to bring home.

Listening 2 (for lower levels)

- Tell students to cover the statements in Exercise 1. They then hear seven of the ten statements on cassette and tick which ones were mentioned.

1 j (little boy) **2** c (little girl) **3** d (man) **4** f (little boy) **5** h (little girl) **6** g (Italian woman) **7** i (man) **a, b, e** are not mentioned.

- Students listen again and note any differences between what is said in the recording and what is written on their page. The different ones are:

> **2C** When my mother's angry with me she she doesn't have a she doesn't have an angry face.
>
> **4f** My mother's the most beautiful person in the world.
>
> **5h** I don't see my mommy very often.
>
> **6g** The mother is the most important person in the family.

2 Fact file

- In groups, students divide up the facts into three or four categories, e.g. 'shocking', 'scientific', though each fact can belong to more than one category. Students can decide on their own categories, but one must be 'false', i.e. it should contain those statistics which are not true. By doing this categorisation, students will be encouraged to discuss the subjects in hand.

Only 10 is false. It should be great-great-great grandmother.

Song
Universal Mother by Sinead O'Connor

DAY 7 Mother's Day

1 Mummy, mom, mama

a I always go to my mother when I have any problems.

b My mother is my best friend.

c Even when she's angry, she doesn't look at me with an angry face.

d I don't think I would want her living with me when she gets older.

e She understands me better than I understand myself.

f She is the most beautiful woman in the world.

g My mother is the most important person in the house.

h I don't see my mother very often.

i She doesn't approve of my partner.

j She shouts a lot.

This is Mum.

Karis Ellen

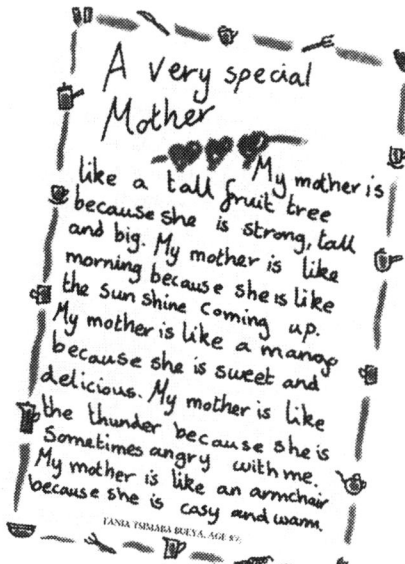

A very special Mother

My mother is like a tall fruit tree because she is strong, tall and big. My mother is like morning because she is like the sun shine coming up. My mother is like a mango because she is sweet and delicious. My mother is like the thunder because she is sometimes angry with me. My mother is like an armchair because she is easy and warm.

TANIA TSIMARA BUEYA, AGE 87.

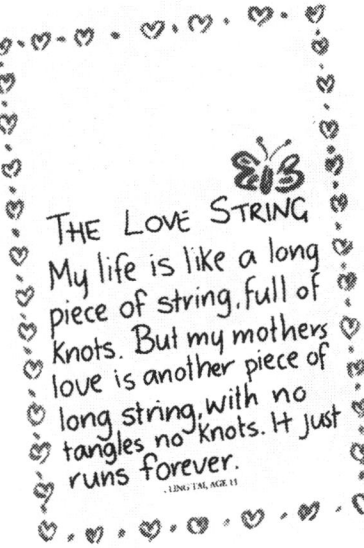

THE LOVE STRING
My life is like a long piece of string, full of knots. But my mothers love is another piece of long string, with no tangles no knots. It just runs forever.

. LING TAI, AGE 11

my mummy

Ciara Pike-Burke

2 Fact file

1 On Mother's Day in 1990 a number of women received medals from the French President as a celebration of their motherhood. Each of the women had borne eight or more children. Mother's Day was being given a political role to heighten awareness of the need to renew a falling population.

2 Commercial surrogacy, when a woman has a child for another woman, is becoming increasingly common in the US.

3 After fertility treatment, Arceli Keh (California) gave birth to a daughter in 1996 at the age of 63. In 1956, before the era of artificial insemination, Ruth Kistler (USA) gave birth when she was 57 years old. The youngest age at which a mother has given birth is 9 years old.

4 Most first-time mothers in the West are in their mid to late 20s.

5 800,000 children are born yearly to US mothers addicted to drugs. Some people say such mothers should be legally prosecuted and jailed.

6 The more educated women are, the less children they have.

7 Leontina Albina (Chile) is the world's most prolific mother (55 children), whereas Geraldine Broderick (Australia) had 9 children all at once (nonuplets).

8 8 to 24-month-old babies (both girls and boys) prefer playing with their father than their mother.

9 Human mothers have much weaker 'maternal instincts' than other animals.

10 The youngest great-great-great-great grandmother: Harriet Holmes (Canada), aged 88.

DAY 8 Easter

Date	March/April
Level	Ex 1 intermediate
	Ex 2 lower intermediate
	Ex 3 upper intermediate
	Ex 4 intermediate
Ages	Exs 1 and 2 all ages
	Exs 3 and 4 mature teenagers and adults
Time	Ex 1 15 minutes
	Ex 2 5 minutes
	Ex 3 15 minutes
	Ex 4 10 minutes
Advice	Exs 1 and 2 are more suitable for Christians.
Vocabulary	Maundy Thursday, ritual, drench, duck (v), crucify, betray, resurrection, crucifixion, pagan, priest, disciple, preach, fertility, tomb, hunt, Palm Sunday, bury, Sabbath, Good Friday, temptation, curse, humility, stone (v), nail, shaman, psychic surgeon

Like most Christian religious festivals, Easter has a pagan origin. The word itself comes from the goddess of rebirth, fertility and spring, the Saxon *Eostre* and Old German *Eostre* (hence the modern German *Ostern*). It is also allied to 'east' from the increasing sunlight and warmth of spring, and to *oster* meaning 'to rise'. This symbolism of rebirth coincided perfectly with Christ's resurrection, and so was easy to adopt into the Christian calendar. The newly converted were able to retain some of their old traditions, including hot cross buns. The bun had originally represented the moon, and the cross divided it into its four 'quarters'. Until quite recently Easter was a much more important event than Christmas.

Other European languages have a completely different word for Easter: Danish *Paske*, French *Pâques*, Icelandic *Paskadagur*, Italian *Pasqua*, Spanish *Pascua*, Portuguese *Pascoa*. All these words come from the Hebrew *pasach* meaning 'passage' or Passover. Passover is a solemn Hebrew festival in celebration of the Israelites' crossing of the Dead Sea while fleeing from Egypt (Exodus 15.1) and lasts seven days. It was celebrated on the 14th day of their first month, so when Christians set their date for Easter (in 325 AD) they avoided having it on the 14th day after the vernal equinox so as to disassociate themselves from the Jews. In any case, Easter cannot be earlier than March 23 or later than April 25. The Orthodox Easter usually falls on a different day, though back in 1963 the Vatican tried unsuccessfully to fix a date for all Christian denominations.

1 Easter traditions

- Elicit what Easter celebrates. (Christ's resurrection.)
- Hand out photocopies and ask students to look at the illustrations. See if they can work out what is happening without reading the texts below.
- Then get them to check by reading the texts and matching them to the illustrations.
- Ask students about their Easter traditions.

 **1** b   **2** d   **3** e   **4** c   **5** a

Listening 1

- Students hear about the origin of Easter eggs. Brainstorm beforehand to see what the class already knows, then dictate the following true/false statements for them to answer.
- **1** Easter eggs have a pre-Christian origin.
- **2** Eggs were forbidden during Lent.
- **3** Chocolate eggs are a recent invention.
- **4** Egg rolling is very popular in Scotland.
- **5** Egg rolling was introduced by the Church.

 **1** T   **2** T   **3** T   **4** T   **5** F

Eggs have always been prominent around this season and most ancient civilisations regarded them as the seed of life and fertility. The Egyptians, Chinese, Greeks and Persians all coloured eggs for their friends. During Lent eggs and other food were forbidden, but at Easter they were given as presents to family, friends and servants. Chocolate eggs are only a fairly recent invention, and in many parts of Britain and America parents hide them for their children to hunt.

A national pastime in Scotland, where Easter Monday used to be known as Egg Monday, is egg rolling. The idea is to see whose egg will reach the bottom of a hill without breaking. The Christian church managed to adapt this pagan ritual by explaining that it represented the rolling away of the tomb where Christ had been buried. In Avenham Park in Lancashire, England, the annual egg-rolling competition attracts up to 40,000 people a year.

Film/song

Jesus Christ Superstar (1973)

2 Easter quiz

- This is only suitable for students from a Christian country, believers and non-believers alike. They can do the quiz in pairs or groups.

 1 Christ's entry into Jerusalem.

(The New Testament tells us that Christ entered Jerusalem on a donkey, but for many years South Americans learned that he entered on a rabbit. This was because the original Spanish missionaries were unable to explain what a donkey was, as the continent had no horses or donkeys. So they described the animal as having long ears – like a rabbit in fact.)

2 Christ's resurrection.

3 The place where Christ was praying when he was arrested.

4 Judas, with a kiss.

5 Christ's crucifixion.

6 He ascended into Heaven.

7 The person who carried Christ's cross.

8 The place where Christ was crucified.

DAY 8 Easter

1 Easter traditions

a Easter is the most important festival of the year in Greece. When the church bells ring at midnight the people proclaim *Christos anesti* – Christ is risen. The squares are filled with people carrying lighted candles. They eat and drink because they have been fasting for forty days. It is traditional for families to return to their home village and barbecue a whole lamb with their relatives. On Easter Monday people have picnics in the parks and fields.

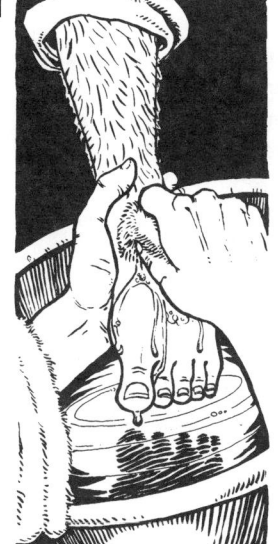

c Children in Latvia hunt for their Easter eggs in the garden. The Easter hare brings chocolate bunnies. The children also have egg-rolling contests.

d In Hungary village boys used to duck the girls in streams or fountains on Easter Monday. Now they just sprinkle the girls with perfume or eau-de-cologne for good luck and good health. The girls then give the boys eggs or invite them to their house for a meal which the girls themselves prepare and serve.

b On Maundy Thursday in Armenia priests wash the feet of 12 chosen boys, just as Christ washed the feet of his disciples. In Belgium a similar ritual takes place on 12 poor old men, who are also given bread and alms. In Britain the King or Queen distributes money to poor people who have given a lifetime's support to their church or community.

e It is dangerous to be in Poland on Easter Monday because you might get drenched in the street or in your car with buckets of water thrown from windows, or even in bed at home. This *œmigusdyngus* custom may have originated around 1000 years ago when thousands of Poles were baptised all together in acceptance of Christianity.

2 Easter quiz

1 What does Palm Sunday, the Sunday before Easter, celebrate?
2 What does Easter Sunday commemorate?
3 What was Gethsemane?
4 Who betrayed Christ, and how?
5 What does Good Friday commemorate?
6 What happened to Christ 40 days after Easter?
7 Who was Simon of Cyrene?
8 What was Calvary?

3 The Crucifixion

- Hand out photocopies and focus students' attention on the photos. Elicit what is happening and what country it might be in.

Listening 2

- Students listen for interest, as if it were a radio programme. (The interview with Pete Forster, half Filippino, is authentic.) They then write two or three questions to ask each other, e.g. Do you think this kind of activity is excessive and do you have any equivalents in your own country? What do you think of missionaries? What do you know about voodoo? Have you ever read or seen anything about psychic surgeons before?

A Tonight *One World* takes a look at an incredible ritual that takes place in the Philippine Islands at Easter. First we're going to listen to a recording I made earlier with an American friend of mine, Pete Forster. And then we're going to discuss what Pete says with our expert, Jan Phillips.

B Good evening, Jeff.

A Good to have you back, Jan. Well, let's hear what Pete has to say.

C What I'm going to relate to you the best that I can remember happened a while back when I was about thirteen years old and we went to the Philippines Islands, the Badjo district of the Philippines, with my mother. It's called the Crucifixion. Because what happens is all the young men of the town vie to be picked to be the person crucified. It's a great honor to be picked to be crucified and ninety per cent of the people that are picked die from it. But they still consider it an honor to their family, to their ancestors, and for themselves to be chosen. Because what happens is they take the individual, they'll stone him, such as they did Jesus, they put the thorn, the wreath of thorns around the head, and they literally crucify him on a cross. And then they parade him down the streets. And it's pretty much sacrificing their life for their belief.

A So, was Pete having me on Jan?

B Not at all, though I don't think as many as ninety per cent die.

A Why the Philippines? Are there many Christians living there?

B Well, actually the Philippines has the biggest Catholic following in Asia, nearly forty million believers. In fact it was the Spanish who, on Easter Day in 1521, began their conquest of the islands with a celebration of the Catholic mass. Missionaries then marched with the armies and converted the Filipinos to Christianity, and often forcibly with swords and whatever.

A But did they manage to stamp out the old beliefs?

B No, not really. In fact, as they did elsewhere, the missionaries had to absorb various pagan elements to make the new religion attractive to potential converts. Still today on some islands Catholicism and paganism exist side by side. There are still shamans who practise all kinds of magic, vodooism even, using human bones, animal sacrifices, offerings to the spirit of the river ...

A And is that where the famous 'psychic surgeons' come from?

B That's right. They say that they can do serious medical operations with just their bare hands.

4 The Holy Bible

- Tell students that the seven events/facts on the Students' Page are either written directly in the Bible or have been interpreted as such by Bible historians and others. Be careful to inform students that not all Christians believe the same things. Fundamentalists, for example, interpret the Bible very literally, others much more liberally. Students' task is to put the texts in order of how certain they are that the events are true, or, if you prefer, in terms of how likely it is that the events really happened. Ensuing discussion should concern such things as the Big Bang, faith healing, myths, etc. Non-Christians can discuss what similarities their religion has with the events/facts that they have read here.

ℹ

You can find further comments on these statements on page 106 in the Appendix.

3 The Crucifixion

Crucifixion: A painful and slow means of execution that the Romans adopted from the Phoenicians. The victim usually died after two or three days. The process of dying included thirst, exhaustion, exposure, and finally, asphyxiation. The hands were often nailed to the crossbeam, which was then hoisted up and affixed to the upright, to which the feet were then nailed.

A peg, astride which the victim sat, supported the main weight of the body. Death was sometimes hastened by breaking the legs, but not in Christ's case.

4 The Holy Bible

1 The world was created in six days by God in 4004 BC.

2 Adam was the first human being and he lived for 930 years in order to father many children.

3 About 4500 years ago, God decided that the earth was corrupt and full of violence, so He flooded it. The only people He saved were Noah and his family, who He had told to build an ark and to collect couples of animals to put on it so that they would be saved.

4 About 3500 years ago, God gave Moses ten commandments in the form of stone tablets regarding the most important things believers must and must not do.

5 About 2000 years ago, Mary became miraculously pregnant through the Holy Ghost and gave birth to the Son of God, Jesus Christ.

6 During his lifetime Jesus performed around 35 miracles, including: walking across water, turning water into wine, curing the blind and the dumb, transforming five loaves of bread and two fishes into enough food for 5000 people, and bringing people back from the dead.

7 Jesus was crucified for insisting that he was the Son of God. He died and was buried. He was then resurrected (brought back to life), before finally going to Heaven to meet his Father.

DAY 9 April Fools' Day

Date	April 1
Level	Ex 1 intermediate
	Ex 2 upper intermediate
Age	all ages, especially teenagers
Time	Ex 1 20 minutes
	Ex 2 20 minutes
Grammar	Ex 2 modals of permission and obligation
Vocabulary	fool, Druid, evacuate, contaminated, practical joke, painstakingly, gravitational pull

April Fools' Day is a day on which people play practical jokes on each other. It became popular in Britain in the 18th century, although its exact origins have not been established. It may have originated in the Roman festival of Hilaria or in the Celtic celebrations of their god Lud. Some date the festival back to Noah's mistake of sending out a dove from the ark before the flood water had gone down – it was a fool's errand to try and find land when the earth was still covered in water and fish. In fact in France children stick fish on each other's back, though the French 'poisson' (fish) may originally have been 'passion', in memory of Christ's passion and how people mocked him on the cross.

Possibly the most likely explanation dates back to 1582 when Pope Gregory XIII ordered the calendar to be changed, so that the new year would begin on March 25 instead of January 1. Anyone who forgot that the date of the new year had changed would be the victim of a practical joke on April 1 – the day when the old new year festivities ended. Since then in England people have been playing incredible practical jokes on each other, including the media. But don't forget – April Fools' tricks are only valid till 12.00 in Britain.

April 1 is celebrated in many countries, including Russia, where they call it *Yumorina* (as in 'humour'), Turkey *Bir Nisan* (simply April the first), and in India the festival of Holi, where children play tricks such as putting salt in tea and firing water pistols at each other. In parts of South and Central America they celebrate Innocents' Day (December 28) which commemorates when King Herod killed the children. Nowadays children play jokes on adults.

1 All Fools' Day

- Don't mention anything about April Fools' Day yet and don't give out any photocopies. With a serious face, ask students whether they have read about the British government's decision to cancel three days in April. Obviously no one will have heard anything (unless you have secretly let one or two students in on the joke and have primed them to say that they read about it in the paper or heard it on TV).

Listening 1
- Students listen to a spoof recording, which you can claim you recorded off the radio.

... said a spokesperson from Downing Street, though the Prime Minister hasn't confirmed this as yet. And yet more problems for the government, this time due to Daylight Saving. The Home Secretary announced yesterday that three days will have to be cancelled next month. She explained that since the introduction of Daylight Saving Time, miscalculations have been made when putting the clocks back, with the result that Britain is now 72 hours behind the rest of the world. The three days to be cancelled will be April 5th, April 12th and April 13th. Anyone with questions should contact their local DSS department. And now today's international news. In Paris this morning residents read that the Eiffel tower is to be disman ...

- Keep the game up for as long as you can, and then explain that students have been victim to an April Fools' joke. Explain that the joke was actually played by London's Capital Radio on its listeners, who called in by the thousand with queries ranging from whether one man would have to pay his staff for the missing days to whether the sale of a house, due to be completed on one of those days, would still be valid.

- Now hand out photocopies and focus students' attention on the headlines. Below the headlines are nine pieces of text taken from newspaper reports about April 1 hoaxes. In pairs, the students' task is to match the texts to just three of the headlines; there are three texts for each of the three headlines. They then have to put the three texts in order.

> Pollution forces children to leave town: 4, 9, 6
> Planetary movements lead to loss of gravity on earth: 2, 8, 3
> Grow your own instant fresh pasta: 1, 7, 5
> N.B. All these hoaxes really happened. All the other headlines, apart from the one on the Eiffel Tower, are the invention of the author.

- Students choose one of the other headlines and write a short paragraph about it. Ask them to read out their texts to the class and then take a vote on the most original one.

DAY 9 April Fools' Day

1 All Fools' Day

The first of April some do say,
Was set apart as All Fools' Day,
But why the people call it so,
Nor I nor they themselves do know!

China to adopt English as official language

Confirmed: Mars colonised by Druid astronauts in 1700 BC

BRITAIN TO ABOLISH ROYAL FAMILY

Language pills for instant learning

Grow your own instant fresh pasta

Planetary movements lead to loss of gravity on earth

Pollution forces children to leave town

Eiffel Tower to be dismantled

1 A BBC documentary last night showed farmworkers in a village near Lugano collecting spaghetti off trees and sitting down at home to enjoy their freshly picked dinners.

2 Earlier today BBC radio listeners were told that Pluto was going to pass behind Jupiter at exactly 9.47 am and that this would make them feel lighter as there would be a decreased gravitational pull.

3 Hundreds of listeners phoned the BBC claiming that the 'experiment' had really worked: one man said his head had hit the ceiling, and a woman claimed that she had floated around the room with eleven friends.

4 On Athens radio it was announced that the atmosphere had become so contaminated with toxic waste that children would have to be evacuated from the town.

5 Hundreds of viewers phoned the BBC to ask where they could buy the amazing spaghetti trees.

6 The journalist who invented the story was sacked.

7 In reality cameramen had painstakingly hung up around 10 kilos of spaghetti and persuaded residents to climb up ladders and gather it in.

8 Listeners were invited to try jumping up in the air and floating.

9 Some listeners rushed to the parks for safety and many others suffered from shock.

2 You can't fool me

- Before handing out photocopies do the listening exercise below.

Listening 2

- Tell students they are going to hear three people describing April Fools' tricks. When they have listened once they write a brief summary of what they have heard and then compare their summaries in pairs.
- Finally they listen again and decide who has written the most accurate summary.

---

1 On April Fools' Day we play lots of tricks on our teachers. Things like we put cushions underneath the cushion on their chair and when they sit on it it makes a rude noise. We also let off stink bombs in the classroom and put cups of water on top of the door so that when the teacher walks in all the water falls on her head.

2 On April the first my son came home from school with a note in his homework book from his teacher saying that he'd been very naughty at school and that I was to go in and see them the next morning. I was very cross with my son until he started laughing, and then he said 'April Fool'.

3 I did a really cruel one. A friend of mine was waiting to hear about a job. And she'd been waiting for weeks and then I noticed that April Fools' Day was coming up. And so on the, about 11 o'clock in the morning I phoned her up. And I pretended to be American, because this job was in America, a small part in the American movie that she was doing. And I pretended to be one of the producers and I offered her the part. And she [oh no] was just so excited, she completely fell for it, hook, line and sinker. And then at the very end of the conversation after we ... she was talking about money, how much she'd get paid, and I said, 'And oh, by the way, April Fool!'

- Students discuss some of their own pranks.
- Alternatively, they write down some true and false statements either about themselves or their country (or anything else they choose). They then read them out and see which ones their partner manages to fall for.
- Hand out photocopies and tell the students that in the USA there have been some very strange state laws in the course of US history. On their page they have some dating back to the beginning of the twentieth century. Instruct them to match the laws on their page with the cartoon illustrations.

🔑 **1** f **2** i **3** a **4** h **5** g **6** c **7** e **8** b **9** d

- In groups students then decide which of the laws they think were invented by newspapers for April Fools' Day.

🔑 They are in fact all laws which were once passed in the USA. (OK, this is a bit of a cheat, but it is April 1st after all!)

- Students can then invent the most ridiculous laws they can think of – again have a vote for the most original one. Try and ensure that students use modals of permission and obligation while writing their laws.

2 You can't fool me

1 Alabama:

> NO FALSE MOUSTACHES CAN BE WORN IN CHURCH IF IT MAKES PEOPLE LAUGH.

2 Arkansas:

> All automobiles must be preceded by a man carrying a red flag.

3 California:

> PEELING AN ORANGE IN A HOTEL ROOM IS FORBIDDEN.

4 Florida:

> **Clothing must be worn while taking a bath in a bathtub.**

5 Idaho:

> *Fishing for trout from the back of a giraffe is not allowed.*

6 Illinois:

> **ANIMALS CAN BE SENT TO JAIL.**

7 Oregon: .

> ONLY LIVING PEOPLE CAN SERVE ON A JURY.

8 South Carolina:

> Guns must be carried to church.

9 Vermont:

> *Painting a horse is illegal.*

a

b

c

d

e

f

g

h

i

DAY 10 May 1

Date	May 1
Level	intermediate
Age	all ages
Time	Ex 1 15 minutes
	Ex 2 10 minutes
Advice	Political – talks about demonstrations and workers' rights.
Grammar	Ex 1 *used to*
Vocabulary	parade, banner, strike, demonstration, slogan, hero, fascism, injustice, unemployment, kindergarten, May Queen, maypole, goddess, ban

May 1 is International Labour Day. While researching this book I found some conflicting evidence as to the origins of this Labour Day: the information in the listening exercise is just one version. In the UK, International Labour Day is not celebrated, but rather May Day, which is connected with folklore rites – maypoles, May Queens, morris dancers, village fairs – and is one of the few occasions when a few daring people dress up in 'traditional' clothes. In the past the girl elected May Queen was not necessarily happy, because although her winning brought good luck to the whole of her village, it was believed that she would die within a year.

1 International Labour Day

- Ask the class whether they celebrate May 1.
- Hand out photocopies and ask students to read the texts which explain what went/goes on in Eastern Europe and what happens today in Germany and Italy.
- Students can then discuss what they would like to protest about on May 1, whether the best workers should be rewarded by the government, and whether they like military parades.
- Alternatively, in groups, students compile a list of workers' rights. They then discuss whether workers in their company or country have these rights, and if not, what would be the best ways of achieving them.
- If students are interested in this topic, then continue with Day 17: Reunification Day, which is dedicated to ex-communist (socialist) countries.

Listening

- Students hear about the origins of International Labour Day. Dictate the following true/false statements for them to answer.
1 The labour holiday certainly began in Australia.
2 In 1886 an American labour federation was campaigning for a shorter working day.
3 On May 3 police killed six demonstrators in Milwaukee.
4 In Chicago eight policemen were killed.
5 The first global labour holiday was in 1819.

May 1 is traditionally an opportunity for workers to express their grievances. Some people believe that it all began in Australia in 1856 with a series of annual strikes. A more likely origin took place thirty years later in 1886 when an American federation of labor called for nationwide strikes and demonstrations for an eight-hour day. On May 1 the police opened fire on a crowd of demonstrators in the city of Milwaukee. Nine people were killed. Two days later in Chicago police killed six demonstrators at a factory in Chicago, though eight of their own men were subsequently killed in the protests which followed.

In July 1889, as part of centenary celebrations of the French Revolution, an international labor congress meeting in Paris called for an international day of demonstrations in support of the eight-hour day on May 1, 1890. And on that date the world celebrated its first global labor holiday.

2 May Day

- Students read the text (based on an interview I did with a kindergarten teacher in Hale, Cheshire, England) and then discuss the following questions.

1 How important is it to learn about other religions? Are there any religions you would like to learn more about?
2 Are any of your festivals of pagan origin? Do you have any similar village celebrations to England's May Day?
3 Have village festivals changed very much since your parents' and grandparents' time?

Follow-up

- For many people May 1 is just a public holiday. Compile a selection of things to do on May 1 (perhaps based on adverts/announcements for sports events, fairs, picnics, demonstrations). In groups, students' task is to reach a consensus on what they would all like to do together on May 1.

DAY 10 May 1

1 International Labour Day

❝ In Russia on May 1 we used to have a parade, even in the smallest villages. You had to go and if you didn't you might have problems at school or work. They used to carry banners with portraits of the heroes of the revolution or slogans. Then there would be announcements about which factory had produced the most, or who was the most efficient worker. In some towns there were military parades too. It was really good fun and then there were plays in the theatre. And at the end of the day everyone was drunk! ❞

(Eugenie Hupar, Russia)

❝ On May 1 in Italy we used to have political demonstrations, generally to defend workers' rights, but more recently they have been to help the waves of immigrants from North Africa and Eastern European countries. ❞

(Andreina Marchesi, Italy)

❝ May 1 demonstrations here in Germany used to be about fighting against fascism, capitalism, social injustice, unemployment, and the exploitation of women and third world countries. But now, unfortunately, many people seem to prefer violence to political protest. ❞

(Peter Erhard, Germany)

2 May Day

May Day in England is celebrated in village fairs where residents dress up in traditional country clothes and dance and sing around a maypole. A May Queen is crowned from the most beautiful girls in the village and this is often followed by much drinking and eating. However, in some parts of the country some Christian parents regularly ban their children from participating in the traditional May Day celebrations, because they say that children dancing round a maypole with flowers round their neck is a pagan rite. (It originated from a Roman festival dedicated to Flora, goddess of flowers and fruit.)

Such parents also complain that their children learn too much about festivals from other religions such as the Jewish Passover, the Muslim Eid-Ul-Fitr, the Chinese Lantern Festival, or the Hindu Holi. But Britain is a multi-racial society and children are encouraged to look for differences and similarities between their festivals, which are all given equal importance. In fact, in kindergartens, nursery schools and primary schools around Britain, as a compulsory part of their school curriculum, children learn the religions and habits of people from many different countries. Indian mothers, for example, will come to the school especially dressed in their saris so that the children can see the different clothes people use.

Day 11 Buddha's Birthday

Date	April/May
Level	upper intermediate
Age	adult
Time	25 minutes
Advice	Students need to have a good knowledge of religious terms and be prepared to talk about their own religion.
Vocabulary	enlightenment, fast (v), meditate, preach, rebirth, enlightenment, Karma, disease, Mantra, tolerance, reincarnation, sinner, pray, butcher, yogi

This unit is primarily aimed at more adult and advanced students. There are many types of Buddhism and this unit is based on interviews with Tibetan and Japanese Buddhists.

Buddha's birthday is celebrated in different countries on different dates – in Japan on April 8, but in most other countries in May. In Thailand the *Visikha Puja*, which celebrates the birth of Buddha, coincides with the full moon, and consists of a candlelit procession.

Buddhism is a philosophy which was originally conceived by Siddharta Gautama (563–483 BC). He was an Indian prince, and, although he was extremely rich, he deeply felt the suffering that was around him. One day, when he was 29, he saw four things that were to change his life: a very old man with a stick, a sick man, a dead man and finally a monk who was resting calmly. He started to ask questions about the meaning of life, but he could find no satisfactory answers. He decided to leave his palace and all his riches. For six years he lived the life of an ascetic, fasting and depriving himself of any pleasures, and even inflicting pain on himself. But he had no success until he began meditating under the sacred Bo-tree, where he tried to find his own solution to the problems of life, disease, suffering and death. After 49 days, he found his answers and he became known as Gautama, the Buddha – the Enlightened One.

In India Buddhism initially dominated over Hinduism, but had been reabsorbed by the fourteenth century. Buddhism became most popular in Tibet, Korea, China and Japan, and also spread to many other parts of the East. It is now becoming popular amongst new agers and alternative people in the West – Richard Gere (the actor), Tina Turner (the singer), Herbie Hancock (the jazz pianist), and Tiger Woods (the golfer) have done a lot, directly and indirectly, in the US to promote Buddhism.

Elements of Buddhism

Listening 1

- Before handing out photocopies, play the recording of a Buddhist monk chanting and see if students can recognise what it is.

- Now brainstorm to find out what students know, if anything, about the origins of Buddhism (see information above). Hopefully, some of your students will have read Hermann Hesse's wonderful book *Siddharta*.

- Hand out photocopies and ask the class to read the statements about Buddhism and answer the following questions, which you dictate to them, or show on an overhead projector.

Which point ...

1 do you agree with the most?
2 do you find most difficult to accept?
3 is impossible to understand? (from a linguistic or conceptual viewpoint)
4 is the most interesting?
5 is most similar/dissimilar to your own religion?

- Alternatively, students could go through each point and compare it to their own religion. This should lead into a discussion of religion in general.

- Finally, focus students on point 10, which implies vegetarianism (something that most students find interesting) and which leads on to the listening.

Listening 2

- Students hear the story of a butcher in Tibet. The moral of the story is that what counts above anything else is sincerity and humility.

- Play the story once or twice. In pairs students try to reconstruct the story and invent a moral for it, with one student writing it down. They then compare their story with another pair's, and make any adjustments. Finally, they listen again and check their stories.

- Get feedback on the moral of the story.

There was this butcher and he had to kill a sheep. But before he killed it he had a few other jobs to do. When he came back, he found that his knife had disappeared. Where had it gone? He looked everywhere for it. He said to himself, 'I'm sure the knife was here. No one is here. The only thing here is the sheep. It must have been her.' So he lifted up the sheep. And there under the ground was buried the knife, and the sheep had been sleeping on top. And the butcher thought to himself, 'What an intelligent animal. She knew I was going to kill her. What a big sinner I am. I kill sheep every day. I'd rather kill myself.' So he throws himself off the top of the mountain. And he flies away.

On the side of the mountain there's a yogi, who sees the butcher flying. And he says to himself, 'What's this? Every day this man kills sheep and, look, he's flying now. I've been here on the mountainside for years, meditating and meditating. If he can fly, then why can't I?' So he throws himself off and goes splat straight down to the ground. Dead.

Films

Tina (in which the singer explains her conversion), *Little Buddha*
Seven Years in Tibet

DAY 11 Buddha's Birthday

Elements of Buddhism

1 *There is not just one form of Buddhism. Buddhism is practised in very different ways in different parts of the world.*

2 Buddhism is not opposed to other religions. A right teaching is right regardless of who preaches it. Truth is truth regardless of who proclaims it.

3 **Buddhism has never caused wars and has always been peacefully introduced around the world.**

4 There is no omnipotent supernatural god in Buddhism – Buddhists look inside themselves, not to any higher being. Heaven and hell are inside us, not outside us.

5 The final goal is to free oneself from the cycle of birth and re-birth and to reach Nirvana (a state of impersonal reality).

6 Actions in the current life have consequences in future reincarnations – the doctrine of Karma. You reap what you sow, you get back what you give.

7 *Enlightenment is something that all human beings can aspire to in their lifetime.*

8 **Suffering, although essential, can be overcome by learning our own potential to resolve difficulties, by believing in the power of positive thinking (through prayer and chanting).**

9 One of the early aims of Buddhism was to create a happy land where people live all their long life free from evil and worry. This is still true today as Buddhists hope to find a world harmony by following natural law.

10 *Some Buddhists claim that many of the remarkable advances in science and technology are actually restricting our freedom, as we depend too much on them. We often leave the cures to doctors rather than preventing or fighting diseases ourselves.*

11 Buddhism preaches non-violence, love of all nature (one must not kill any living creature), equality of all men and women, respect for the individual, and tolerance.

12 Some Buddhists in the West believe that through chanting particular Sanskrit verses, you can get whatever it is you want – a new job, a new house, a partner. The same chanting can help you face violence and death.

DAY 12 Children's Day

Date	varies
Level	intermediate
Age	teenagers
Time	25 minutes
Grammar	modals of obligation: *should, have to, would*
Vocabulary	chore, amazing, gift, tell off, amusement park, kids, party, dolls, weapons, carp

ⓘ

Sadly, few cultures have a day dedicated to children. Japan seems to be the only country that goes in for honouring children in a big way. They have a Coming-of-Age Day (*Seijin-no-hi,* January 15), Girls' Festival (*Hina-matsuri,* March 3), Boys' Festival (*Kodomo-no-hi,* May 5) and a festival for children aged 3, 5, and 7 (*Shichi-go-san,* November 15). Other countries in the East and in Africa, which have either been recently created or have had a radical change in government, also have their Children's Days or Youth Days (e.g. Singapore and South Africa). These cases seem to be recent attempts by governments to create a sense of responsibility in the new youth who will be the inheritors of the hard work that the government has done in trying to create a sense of national unity and pride. One of my references claims that the second Sunday in June is celebrated as Children's Day in the USA (hence the location of this Day in this book), though no American I know has ever heard of it. Apparently it was first celebrated in the mid 1800s by Protestants, who christened children on this day.

Boys and girls

- Ask students whether they have a Children's Day in their country, and, if so, what it consists of. If they don't have a Children's Day, they could hypothesise on *why* they don't have one. Brainstorm about how, if there *was* a Children's Day, it could be celebrated. Write their suggestions on the board, eliciting, if possible, some of the ideas mentioned in the Listening exercise.

Listening

- Play extracts 1 and 2 – adults saying how they imagine Children's Day would be. Ask the class to list the suggestions the adults make, and then say whether they agree with them or not.

- Now play extracts 3, 4 and 5. Students then see whether this English boy's and the two American girls' ideas coincide with their own (i.e. those you've written on the board in the pre-listening activity).

▄▄▄

1 I think they should be able to have breakfast in bed to start the day. And then that they should be able to select their ... the programs on the television that they would like to watch. And should be able to demand one chore from each of the parents within reason. I don't think they

should be able to select their food, because then they would just make pigs of theirselves.

2 Children should *definitely* not have to go to school on that day. Presents would be in order, if they gave children gifts, and maybe a card for being good throughout the rest of the year.

3 Well, Children's Day, I think it would be an amazing thing if it actually happened. There definitely should be no school. They should be bought sweets, everything, presents, they should be given money. Everything. Television. Television should be just taken over by kids' programmes, kids' films. Cinemas should be free. There should be fairs opened. I think parents should not be allowed to tell their children off on that particular day.

4 What I would do if there was a Children's Day, I would basically just run free because I would just go places without having to check in with my parents or without them supervising me or asking if I can go some place, just go.

5 I'd have a party, a huge party with all my friends, and I'd party all day and all night.

- Now hand out the photocopies and ask students to read the texts and answer the questions. They could do this in small groups initially and you could have a final round-up discussion with the whole class.

- Alternatively you could set one of the questions as written work.

Follow-up

- Ask students to define what a good parent (or child) should be like – the kind of things they should (not) be allowed to do, should have to do, etc.

DAY 12 Children's Day

Boys and girls

In Mexico all the movies are half price or free on Children's Day, and the parks too. Adults give children presents – toys, clothes and candy. Children really look forward to it.

(Claudia Cano, Mexico)

In Japan we have two big secular festivals for children – one for girls and one for boys, on different days. This division is part of Japanese tradition. In fact until the Second World War they thought that girls and boys shouldn't play and study together after the age of seven. We can see this difference in the two festivals. On the girls' day, which is not a national holiday, the girls play with special dolls which they keep and display until they are married. On the boys' day, which is also known as Children's Day, there is no school. Boys show off weapons and fly banners of carps – the carp is a symbol of strength, as it is a fish which can swim upstream.

(Yoshie Kojima, Japan)

We have Children's Day in June. We have parties at school and then we go on excursions with our teachers. All the amusement parks are free on this day.

(Lucia Oliveira Noversa, Portugal)

In the US we don't have a Children's Day. Some people wanted to organise a national day for children, but they were told that children were celebrated every day, so there was no need for one. But I think there should be one.

(Natashia Hancock, USA)

It would be good to have a special day when children could say what they really think about things, because parents, and adults in general, make a lot of decisions involving us without ever asking us.

(Andrew Brogdon, Great Britain)

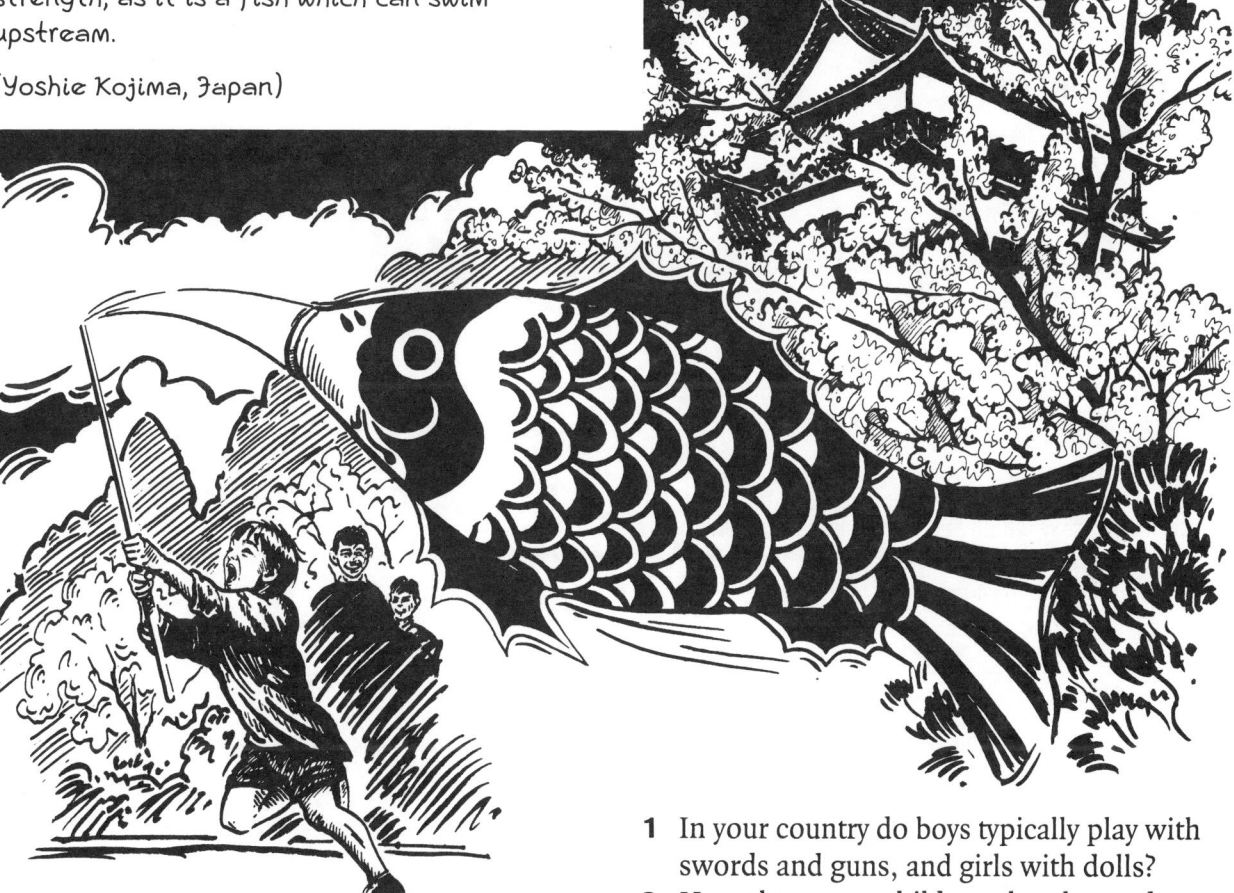

1 In your country do boys typically play with swords and guns, and girls with dolls?
2 Have the games children play changed much over the last 100 years? And in the last 20 years?
3 How has the role of children changed over the years?

DAY 13 Father's Day

Date	UK/US: 3rd Sunday in June
	Catholics: March 19
Level	intermediate
	Listening 2 upper intermediate
Age	all ages
	Listening 2 adults
Time	Ex 1 15 minutes
	Ex 2 25 minutes
Advice	Listening 2 questions traditional male roles.
Vocabulary	honour, Civil War veteran, raise kids, worthy, virtue, inheritance, evil, heritage, sexist, paternity leave, discretion, provide for, bring up children, short-sighted

In the UK the third Sunday in June passes almost unnoticed (and is probably no more than a money-spinning import from the US), but in many Catholic countries March 19 (St Joseph's Day) is quite a big event. Joseph was of course the human father of Christ, hence the choice of day for celebrating fathers. Valencia, in Spain, goes in for massive Father's Day celebrations where *fallas* (bonfires) are the main feature. *Fallas* artists fashion grotesque or satiric images of animals, houses, gods or humans, which are then located round the town for people to admire. This is followed by bullfights, parades, fireworks, etc. All the images are burnt apart from the winning one.

1 Father and son

- Ask students what they do, if anything, on Father's Day. What is the best kind of present to get one's father?

Listening 1

- Students hear an American girl and a Spanish girl saying what happens on Father's Day in their countries (authentic recordings). Ask further comprehension questions if you wish. Put the following headings on the board (without the answers!) and ask students to listen and fill in the table.

	Date	Origin	Cards?	Gifts?
America	3rd Sunday June	veteran's daughter	yes	yes
Spain	March 19	Joseph	yes	yes

1   Father's Day in the US came about similar to Mother's Day and it's a day set aside for everyone's father, to honor them and give thanks, and usually give small little gifts or cards to your father. And ... how it came about is a woman wanted to honor her father who was a Civil War veteran, who had to raise six kids on his own because his wife was dead. It takes place on   the third Sunday of June and that's Father's Day and usually around a hundred million Father's Day cards are sent annually in the US, which is fifty million less than on Mother's Day.

2   In Spain we celebrate Father's Day on the nineteenth of March. And it's a very important holiday because, as Saint Joseph was the father of Christ, we celebrate Father's Day and give presents to our fathers and also to people whose name is Joseph and also Josephine, if it's a woman. We give cards to all these people and also all the family get together to celebrate the date of the father.

- Hand out photocopies and ask students to read the text about the roles and duties of sons and fathers and decide in which country and approximately when they were written. (Thailand, recently.) Students discuss whether they are relevant for themselves. Some of these points may be totally alien to your students, but this in itself should be a source of discussion.
- They should then use this as a basis to formulate a similar set of rules for mothers and daughters.

Song

Cat Stevens' classic *Father and Son*

Films

On Golden Pond, *Father's Day*, *Hamlet*

2 Father's Day quiz

- Students do the quiz individually and then compare their answers. Discussion of these questions obviously implies discussing the role of mothers too.

Listening 2

- Students hear some adults discussing the role of the father today. Their task is to decide which of the sentences in question 5 are touched on/referred to.

 b c g h

You will find the tapescript of this conversation on page 107 in the Appendix.

Follow-up

- Students discuss what kind of father and mother they will be (or already are) compared with their own parents. Will they bring their children up in the same way as they themselves were brought up?

DAY 13 Father's Day

1 Father and son

Roles and duties of sons towards their father

- Support him.
- Work for him.
- Maintain the honour and traditions of the family.
- Make themselves worthy of his heritage.

Roles and duties of fathers towards their sons

- Train them in virtue and keep them away from evil.
- Have them taught arts and sciences.
- Arrange marriage to a suitable wife.
- Provide their inheritance in due time.

2 Father's Day quiz

1 Being a father is most difficult with what age of children?

- a pre-school
- b elementary – middle school
- c high school
- d college
- e adult

2 How responsible are fathers for what their children do?

- a 100%
- b 75%
- c 50%
- d 25%
- e 10%

3 How much time a day should a working father spend with his child?

- a more than three hours
- b two hours
- c an hour or so
- d less than an hour

4 Do you obey your father out of a sense of ...

- a fear?
- b respect?
- c love?
- d habit?

5 Are the following statements true or false?

- a A father should not try to be a friend to his children.
- b The role of fathers has changed more than the role of mothers in the last 100 years, but is still very sexist.
- c Fathers and mothers should keep their roles separate and well defined.
- d In divorce cases fathers should have as much right to the children as mothers.
- e It's easier being a father than a mother.
- f The media, and society in general, give mothers a better image than fathers.
- g Fathers should be entitled to paternity leave.
- h Only fathers should go out to work.

Some dads give them everything except love,
some give them nothing but love.

Aysegul Corecki
Age 15

DAY 14 Summer Solstice

Date	June 21 (Northern hemisphere)
	December 21 (Southern hemisphere)
Level	intermediate
Age	all ages
Time	Ex 1 20 minutes
	Ex 2 20 minutes
Vocabulary	yo-yo, worship, planet, annual pathway, horoscope, temperature, nucleus, fusion test reactor, photosynthesis, oil, coal, tidal, geyser, hot spring, volcano, earthquake

When you do this unit will obviously depend on which hemisphere you live in. The sun and sun worshipping has had an enormous effect on our everyday lives, especially in terms of fixing the religious calendar. Solstice literally means 'standing of the sun' (cf armistice), and the summer solstice occurs when the sun reaches the Tropic of Cancer and the point on the celestial sphere where it is farthest north of the celestial equator, hence giving us our longest day.

In Shakespeare's time June 21 was Midsummer Day/Night. This harks back to a time when the year was divided into two seasons – summer and winter (in fact the Sanskrit word for summer means 'half year'), whereas now many dictionaries define summer as actually beginning on June 21.

Although the summer solstice actually occurs around June 21, in Europe Midsummer Day was celebrated on a fixed day, June 24, just as the winter solstice was celebrated on December 25 rather than December 21. And just as the birth of Christ was fixed at December 25 to quash the old pagan traditions, John the Baptist's birthday was fixed on June 24 to detract pagans from worshipping the sun – from the Druids at Stonehenge in England to the Mayans at Kukukan pyramid in Mexico.

The 'fires of St John' may have originated in the fertility rites of the Druids. Fires were also lit to encourage the sun not to lose its power and as a cure and protection against disease.

On this day the inhabitants of northern towns in Portugal go around hitting each other on the head with plastic hammers and pushing garlic plants under each other's noses! In San Juan in Puerto Rico bonfires are lit on the beaches and people take a swim to commemorate the saint who baptised people in water. French Canadians in Quebec celebrate the Fête de la Saint Jean-Baptiste with parades, bonfires and fireworks.

In Scandinavian countries the sun never really goes down at the summer solstice. Since pagan times in Sweden, Midsommar has been a time of great fun and partying – no one goes to bed!

- Ask your students when they think summer begins and ends (and the other seasons too). Ask them if they celebrate the summer solstice.

1 Sun poems

- Before handing out photocopies, brainstorm with students on the importance of the sun for native people and for our ancestors (e.g. warmth, light, helped them to grow crops, religious symbol).
- Ask students to write a poem entitled 'Sun'. The poem can either be four words long or a series of short verses.
- Ask a few students to read their poems aloud.
- Hand out photocopies and ask students to compare their poems with the ones on the page. Ask them how old they think the poets were and what nationality; also, which verse in the second poem do they like best?

Sun: adult, native American   What is the sun?: age 9   UK

2 Sun quiz

- Ask students to do the quiz in pairs. Some of it will be guesswork.

Listening
- Students hear the answers to the quiz.

 1 T   2 F   3 b   4 c   5 T   6 c   7 a, b, c

Nearly all early civilisations worshipped the sun, for example the inhabitants of Mesopotamia, the Egyptians, Romans, Norsemen, and the Mayans, Aztecs and Incas. In fact some named their days of the week after the planets. They also recognised that the constellations of the Zodiac formed a broad band that seemed to be the annual pathway of the sun. From this they derived all kinds of horoscopes.

What they couldn't have calculated was just how heavy the sun is, about 300,000 times heavier than the Earth. The sun's vast temperature, about 5500 degrees centigrade at the surface and 15 million in the nucleus, would seem to be higher than could ever be reached on Earth. But back in 1994 at a fusion test reactor in the USA, a temperature of 510 million degrees was achieved.

Although the sun is some 150 million kilometres from the Earth, it is responsible for nearly everything that goes on on the Earth – as a life giver to animal and plant life through photosynthesis and as an energy supplier through solar, hydroelectric, oil and coal power. However, it is the moon which is principally responsible for tidal forces; and energy from the Earth's interior causes geysers, hot springs, volcanoes and earthquakes.

Discussion
- Would students prefer to live in a country whose hours of daylight vary very little, or in one which has very long days in the summer and very short days in the winter?

DAY 14 Summer Solstice

1 Sun poems

Sun

hot

round

shiny

high

<u>What is the sun?</u>

The sun is a clock,
Which ticks out heat.

The sun is a pound coin,
Buying more sky.

The sun is a light bulb,
Which lights up our world.

The sun is a sunflower,
Which grows in Heaven's garden.

The sun is a lemon,
In God's fruit bowl.

The sun is an egg,
Feeding the planets.

The sun is a yo-yo,
Bouncing around.

2 Sun quiz

1 True or false? The days Sunday and Monday derive from days dedicated to the sun and to the moon.

2 True or false? The zodiac system, from which horoscopes derive, is governed by the moon, not the sun.

3 How much heavier is the sun than the Earth?
   a about 300 times heavier
   b 300,000 times
   c 300,000,000 times

4 What is the temperature (in degrees centigrade) of the nucleus of the sun?
   a 5500
   b 15500
   c 15 million
   d 150 million

5 True or false? The highest man-made temperature ever achieved was over 30 times hotter than the temperature at the nucleus of the sun.

6 The Earth's distance from the sun is about ...
   a 15,000 km
   b 150,000 km
   c 150,000,000 km
   d 150,000,000,000 km

7 Which of the following are not principally caused by the sun?
   a earthquakes
   b volcanoes
   c tides
   d oil and coal deposits
   e photosynthesis

DAY 15 Independence Day

Date	July 4 (US)
Level	intermediate
Age	all ages
Time	Ex 1　15 minutes
	Ex 2　15 minutes
	Ex 3　10 minutes
Advice	Students may find it strange to talk about the advantages of colonisation.
Vocabulary	grant/gain independence, empire, colony, protectorate, kingdom, republic, monarchy, commonwealth

Most countries have gained independence at some time or other in their history from a foreign power. It would have been impossible to cover everyone's Independence Day, so the days covered here are very much subjective choices.

In 1939 more than 25% of the people in the world lived in parts of European empires. The following countries were once British colonies: USA (1776), Canada (1876), Australia (1901), South Africa (1910), New Zealand (1931). The British Commonwealth was founded in 1931 and is a free association of over 50 independent states with a total population of nearly two billion. Some members still consider the English monarch as their monarch, others have their own monarchs or are republics. The original members were Australia, Canada, Irish Free State, Newfoundland, New Zealand and South Africa (which left in 1961 and rejoined in 1994). Other major members are Bangladesh, India, Jamaica, Kenya, Malaysia, Nigeria, Pakistan (left in 1972 and rejoined in 1989), Singapore, Sri Lanka, Tanzania and Uganda. Members of the Commonwealth have a certain favoured economic status with the UK, and participate in an Olympics-like sports event known as the Commonwealth Games.

1 When and who from?

- Ask students whether their country has at any time been under a foreign power and, if so, when it became independent.

- Hand out photocopies and focus attention on the box with the names of countries. In groups students try and guess which country (i.e. Bulgaria, Finland, etc.) gained independence from whom. If you like, they can also try to guess the date.

- Get feedback and give the answers.

1 Turkey 1908　**2** Russia 1917　**3** Denmark 1944
4 Great Britain 1937　**5** ex-USSR 1990　**6** Sweden 1905
7 France 1953　**8** Great Britain 1947　**9** Holland 1949
10 USA 1946

Listening 1

- As they listen, students look at the map and write in the box who the country gained independence from, and in which year. Some students might like to guess some of the answers before listening.

Argentina 1816 Spain	**Chile** 1818 Spain
Brazil 1822 Portugal	**Uruguay** 1825 Brazil
Syria 1946 France	**Tunisia** 1956 France
Algeria 1962 France	**Libya** 1951 Italy
Iraq 1932 Great Britain	

Argentina, in 1816, was the first country in South America to gain independence from the Spanish, and was followed two years later by Chile. But of course the Portuguese had the biggest single territory, Brazil, which was made independent in 1822. Uruguay, which was part of Brazil, only had to wait another three years before being granted independence by the Brazilians.

European countries had many colonies and protectorates in North Africa and the Middle East. Syria was one of the first to gain independence from the French in 1946, then Tunisia in 1956, and Algeria in 1962. Italy too had colonies in the same region. For example, Libya, which became a kingdom in 1951, and then a republic in 1969. Iraq was a British protectorate for 12 years before becoming an independent monarchy in 1932, though later becoming a republic in 1958.

Follow-up

- Discuss the pros and cons of colonisation, both from the point of view of the colonised country and the colonising country (e.g. a way to get wealth, a way to stop other countries from colonising, a patriotic duty to prove your country was superior, a belief that you could bring the natives a better quality of life). Who would students most/least like to be colonised by?

DAY 15 Independence Day

1 When and who from?

1	Bulgaria
2	Finland
3	Iceland
4	Irish Republic
5	Lithuania
6	Norway
7	Cambodia
8	India
9	Indonesia
10	Philippines

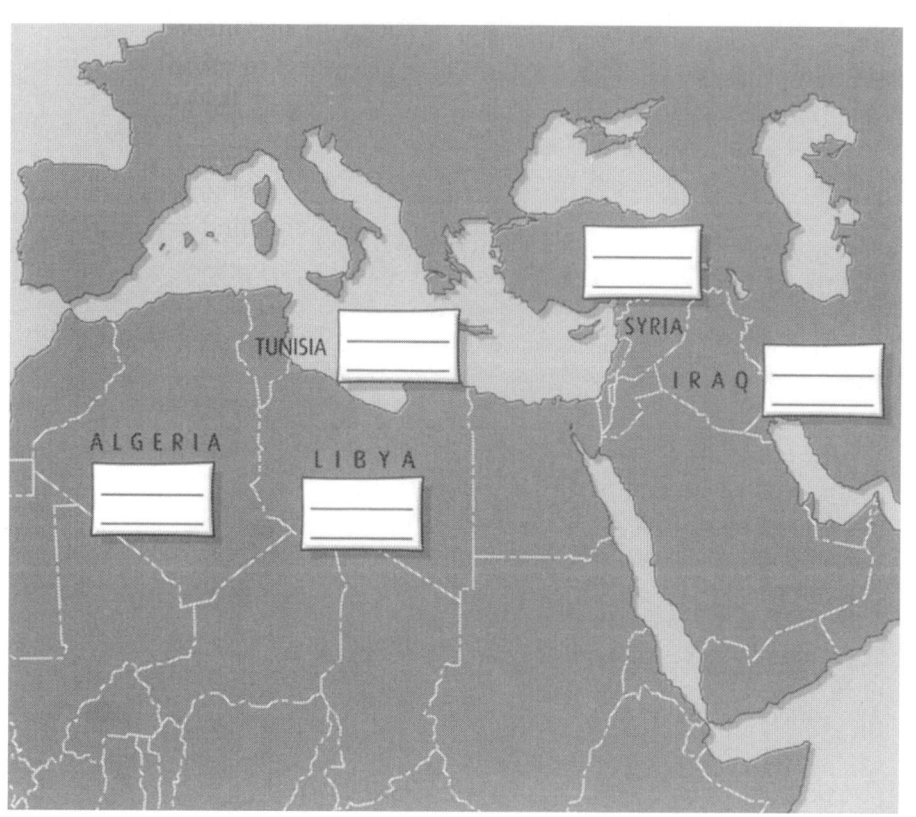

2 July 4

- Hand out photocopies and ask students if, and when, they have a national holiday and what it celebrates. In pairs they complete the first column of the table, ticking those elements that form part of their celebrations.
- Ask if students know why Americans celebrate July 4 and who they are celebrating independence from. Then they read the text.

Listening 2

- Students hear two Americans describing what they do on July 4. They complete the second two columns in the table by ticking the items they hear mentioned.

	Speaker 1	Speaker 2
barbecue/picnic	✔	✔
civil processions		
family get-together	✔	✔
fireworks	✔	✔
flag		✔
formal meal		
military parade		
sport	✔	
street parties		

1 July 4 happens to be America's favorite holiday. It is a time where you can meet with your family. It's a time where you would re-unite with loved ones and pretty much have fun all day long. It's a day in America where it's a festival day, so everyone normally spends time all day long with their family doing things. It's a time where you would meet together and you would barbecue, eat a lot of food, drink a lot of beverages and play a lot of sporting events. If you're older and you're into sporting events, you would normally go to a baseball game at the stadium. And you would spend all day long there. After the game there are fireworks of course that at at at the conclusion of the game and you spend time with your friends and loved ones watching the fireworks.

2 What I usually do for the fourth of July, since it was the day when the United States became a whole country … we usually get together with our other family members, and they usually have the American flag blowing, and then of course we shoot off fireworks and have a little, like we usually have a barbecue since it's in the summer and we just spend it with our family.

3 India

- Students decide whether the statements about India are true or false. They then correct their answers during the listening.

Listening 3

- Students hear the story of India's independence from Britain (August 15 1947).

 **1** F **2** T **3** T **4** F **5** T **6** F **7** F (10 million refugees)

The British Empire was the biggest of the European Empires. In the 1920s and 30s Britain had made part of its Empire into a Commonwealth. Huge countries, like Canada, Australia and New Zealand, had quite small populations dominated by white settlers. They were allowed to rule themselves as independent countries, but with the King of England as the Head of State. India was the 'Jewel in the Crown' of the British Empire. It was the richest colony, with an enormous population, far greater than that of Britain.

The Indian people wanted to rule themselves, but Britain refused to treat them like Canada or Australia. Between the two world wars Mahatma Gandhi became the leader of the Indian independence movement. He wanted to use non-violent methods to force the British to grant India independence. He organised strikes and huge protest meetings, as well as campaigns to boycott British goods and to stop paying taxes.

During the Second World War the Japanese threatened to capture India. The Indian Congress Party refused to support Britain in the war, so the British promised them independence once the war was over, if they would join in the war against Japan.

In 1947 Britain gave up control of India. However, the Hindus and Muslims wanted to rule themselves, and so two separate countries were formed, India and Pakistan. There were terrible riots, which left as many as one million dead and led to ten million people becoming refugees.

Films
Gandhi, Heat and Dust or *A Passage to India*

Follow-up
- Ask students to discuss the following questions.
- Are you proud to be a citizen of your country? Why? Why not?
- If you could become a citizen of another country, which country would you choose?
- If you could form a new independent country, what would your aims and ideals be?

2 July 4

	Your country	Speaker 1	Speaker 2
barbecue/picnic			
civil processions			
family get-together			
fireworks			
flag			
formal meal			
military parade			
sport			
street parties			

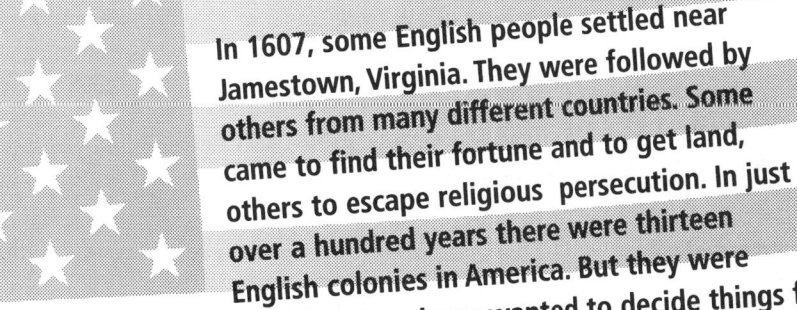

In 1607, some English people settled near Jamestown, Virginia. They were followed by others from many different countries. Some came to find their fortune and to get land, others to escape religious persecution. In just over a hundred years there were thirteen English colonies in America. But they were governed by the King of England. As time passed, the Americans wanted to decide things for themselves. They wanted to make their own laws. Things got worse and worse, and violence erupted. Finally, on April 19, 1775, there was a battle between the Americans and the British soldiers. It was the start of the American Revolution. Initially, they just wanted to defend their rights, but it wasn't long before they wanted to be completely independent. On July 4, 1776, the American leaders approved the Declaration of Independence, stipulating that people had the right to be free. The thirteen colonies united to fight for that freedom but had to wait nearly eight years for peace to come.

3 India

We did not conquer India for the benefit of the Indians. We conquered India as a market for the goods of England. (British Home Secretary, 1928)

True or false?

1 The British Empire was second only in size to the French Empire.
2 Canada, Australia and New Zealand were once part of the British Empire before becoming part of the Commonwealth.
3 India was Britain's richest colony.
4 Mahatma Gandhi wanted to use violence to force the British to grant India independence.
5 During the Second World War the British promised India independence in return for help fighting against the Japanese.
6 Three separate countries – India, Pakistan, and Bangladesh – were formed.
7 Terrible riots left one million dead and led to twenty million people becoming refugees.

DAY 16 Diwali

Date	October/November
Level	Ex 1 intermediate
	Ex 2 upper intermediate
Age	adults
Time	Ex 1 5 minutes
	Ex 2 30 minutes
Advice	Students need to have a good knowledge of religious terms and to be prepared to talk about their own religion.
Vocabulary	exile, prosperity, founder, all-pervasive, reincarnation, philosophy, Aryan, settle, union, sacred, cow, forehead, sari, refrain, consequence, vegetarian

- Hand out photocopies with the Hinduism text at the bottom of the page folded back and tell students not to read it yet.

1 Diwali

- Students read the text for interest.

2 Hinduism

- Ask students, in groups, to read the questions and discuss the answers without reading the text. They then check their answers with the text.

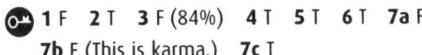 **1** F   **2** T   **3** F (84%)   **4** T   **5** T   **6** T   **7a** F
7b F (This is karma.)   **7c** T

Follow-up

- Focus students' attention on the four pictures: (from L to R) a woman with a dot on her forehead, the four-armed Hindu god Shiva, a Hindu shrine and a sacred cow.

- Students should write down as many questions related to these pictures as they can, imagining that they are going to be answered by a Hindu. Examples: Why has this God got so many arms? Who is he? Do Hindus worship more than one god? Do they worship images and idols? Why do Hindu women have a dot on their forehead? Do only women wear this dot? Why do Hindus regard the cow as sacred? Do Hindus eat meat?

- Ask students to read out their questions, while you write them on the board. Now brainstorm with the class to see what they know about Hinduism and if they can answer any of their own questions. Get them to reason over their answers. Examples: Think of all the possible uses of a cow and why it might be sacred (milk, cream, ice cream, yoghurt, cheese, butter, beef, bones used in soup, leather); imagine life without cows.

- Make sure all the example questions above have been mentioned before proceeding with the listening.

Listening

- Students hear the answers to some of the questions outlined above. Ask them to look at the pictures on their page. With low levels, students should simply try to understand which picture is being talked about; higher levels should also understand the actual answers. Which picture is not talked about? What is talked about but not illustrated?

1 the god Shiva   **2** the sacred cow   **3** the dot on the forehead. The Hindu shrine is not talked about. Vegetarianism is talked about but not illustrated.

1 Hindus worship many hundreds of gods, which represent different aspects of Brahman, but the three most important gods are Brahma the creator, Vishnu the protector and Shiva the destroyer. Shiva is also called the Lord of the Dance, because he is often shown dancing. Dance is a way of showing the energy flowing through the world, which is responsible for life and death, good and evil. Shiva's four hands symbolise his power over these. But he is not a cruel god; the old needs to be destroyed to make way for the new.

2 Hindus regard all living creatures as sacred – mammals, fishes, birds and more. The cow symbolically represents all other creatures to the Hindu. The cow is a good example to man because it is so giving, it gives and gives and gives, like the soul, and takes only grass and grain. In a society with no other domestic animals, we could still survive if we only had the cow.

3 Not only women but also Hindu men wear the dot on the forehead. It indicates their third eye. It also helps to identify a Hindu among members of other religions. If you think about it, Sikhs wear turbans, Muslim women often wear a veil, Christians wear crosses. In many cases the dot is just like a beauty mark, which often complements the colour of a lady's sari.

4 This is a very touchy subject. Basically there is an underlying Hindu rule, called ahimsa, which means refraining from injuring physically or mentally any living creature. This is because the same spirit that unites us all, Brahman, is in us all, so of course not eating meat is a natural consequence. However, there are no commandments, and it's up to Hindus themselves what they put in their body. In fact today only about twenty to thirty per cent of Hindus are vegetarians.

- Discuss any matters arising from the listening, e.g. whether students agree with vegetarianism, should insects be included in those animals that shouldn't be physically harmed?

DAY 16 Diwali

1

Diwali

Diwali is a popular Hindu and Sikh festival, held in the Hindu month of Ashvina (around late October, early November) just before the new moon, when the sky is at its darkest. It is one of the most joyful celebrations – a festival of lights, fireworks and sweets.

At Diwali time people light rows of small lamps (traditionally clay lamps) or candles and put them in their windows and doorways to welcome the god Rama, commemorating his return from exile, which is described in the sacred book, the *Ramayana*.

In preparation for Diwali they clean their homes in the hope that Lakshmi, the goddess of prosperity, will visit them. They wear new clothes and visit friends and relations. They offer sweets to Lakshmi, and, after prayers, the sweets are shared.

Bonfires are lit and there are brilliant firework displays, to show that darkness can be driven away by light, as can evil by good.

2 Hinduism

Which of the following statements are true?

1 Mahatma Gandhi was the founder of the Hindu religion.
2 Hinduism is much older than Christianity and Islam.
3 Hindus only represent about a quarter of the total population of India.
4 Hindus believe in many gods.
5 Hindus believe that there is one all-pervasive God which energises the entire universe.
We can see Him in the life shining out of the eyes of humans and all creatures.
He is not living in some remote heaven but is inside all of us.

6 The goal of every Hindu is to achieve *moksha*, union with Brahman.
7 Reincarnation is an important aspect of Hinduism. It means:
  a not eating cows and other sacred animals.
  b the law of cause and effect, i.e. if I do good things, then good things will happen to me (in this life or in another), but if I do bad things, these bad things will eventually have a negative effect on me/my soul.
  c the idea that your soul never dies, but chooses a series of different bodies to live in until it finally manages to live outside the body.

Fold here

About 84% of the Indian population is Hindu. Unlike other religions, Hinduism is not named after or based on the philosophy of a founder. Around 3500 years ago the Aryans invaded India from the Northwest and settled in the Indus river valley around 1500 BC. The Persians called India 'the land beyond the river Indus' and so the people living there were known as Hindus. The religions of these peoples combined, and in fact, in the course of history, many foreigners came to India and many of their ideas were absorbed by Hindu society. Still today, Hindus do not deny the existence of other gods.

Hindus believe that we can see God, or Brahman, in everything; he is inside us and outside us. A Hindu's ultimate aim is to reach union with Brahman, which is done by a long process of reincarnation. How long this takes depends on your karma – the actions you do and the results they have. A good karma in this life will mean you are reborn into a better life. Reincarnation literally means 're-entering the body' and the soul has to live in lots of different bodies to learn all the different lessons of life. Eventually the soul reaches a state of *moksha*, when it no longer needs a human body to contain it.

DAY 17 Reunification Day

Date	October 3
Level	upper intermediate
Age	mature teenagers and adults
Time	Ex 1 15 minutes
	Ex 2 25 minutes
Advice	This is a political topic, talking about socialism and communism.
Vocabulary	occupation zone, communist, socialist, airlift supplies, strike, democracy, homeless, beggars, Stasi, drugs, takeover

Reunification Day (*Tag der Einheit*) is on October 3 and celebrates the falling of the Berlin Wall and the reunification of East and West Germany.

1 The Berlin Wall

- Brainstorm to find out what students know about the story of the Berlin Wall before, during and after it was built. They then read the text for interest.

Listening

- Dictate the following questions for students to answer.
1 Why was 'communist' not the right word to describe Eastern European countries?

2 What advantages were there of living in East Germany before 1989?

3 What fraction of the East German population acted as informers for the state security police?

4 What were children encouraged to do?

5 Rather than 'reunification' what do some ex-East Germans consider unity with West Germany to be?

1 They called themselves 'socialist'.
  2 Low rents, few homeless people or beggars, high employment for women, good education.
  3 One third.
  4 Spy about TV programmes watched by their neighbours and parents.
  5 A takeover.

A And had life really been so bad during the communist period?

B Communist isn't really the right word. In fact all those countries that we in the West call communist actually called themselves socialist. In fact, if you think about it, the USSR stood for Union of Soviet Socialist Republics, not Communist Republics. But to go back to your question – no. No, it hadn't been so bad. They'd had housing provided for all, with rents fixed at 1939 prices. There were very few homeless people, no beggars on the street like there are now. They had good childcare facilities, which incidentally meant that there were a lot of jobs for women. They had a good education system, some would say better than they've got now ...

A Sounds like a Utopia.

B But of course there's the downside too. There was the dreaded STASI – the state security police, with its network of informers, which made up nearly a third of the population, it was rumoured. Children were encouraged to look into their neighbours' windows to see what they were watching on TV, because they weren't allowed to watch any western movies. And next morning at school the teacher would say, 'What did your mummy and daddy watch last night?'

A Sounds terrible. No freedom at all.

B Yes, but you could argue: what has freedom of choice brought them? Organised crime, beggars, drugs ...

A I've heard some East Germans complain that, rather than reunification with West Germany, what they actually experienced was a takeover.

B I think to some extent that's true. There was certainly a tendency, and not just on the western side, to think that the West is the best, so to speak.

- Alternatively, this listening exercise would make a good introduction to Exercise 2, 'The good old days?'.

THE BERLIN WALL

At the end of World War II Berlin was divided into four sectors by the Americans, British, French and Russians, pending the reunification of Germany by peace treaty. After friction between Soviet and Western commanders, the Soviet occupation zone (East Berlin) split from the other three to become under communist rule in the German Democratic Republic (DDR).

In 1948, with the beginning of the Cold War, the USSR stopped all movement into West Berlin by land. This meant that the West had to airlift supplies to save the city from starvation – between 4000 and 8000 tons of food and other vital supplies a day for 11 months until the blockade ended in 1949. Soon people began crossing from East Berlin to West Berlin, where they either stayed or were flown to the West.

On 13 August 1961 the East Germans began building the wall to prevent such people from leaving – more than 1,500,000 had escaped through Berlin since 1949. The meandering concrete wall was four metres high, lined with barbed wire and protected by an electrified fence. If straightened, it would have been 103 miles long. There were 285 watchtowers with flood lights and manned by guards with machine guns. Few people managed to escape, due to the interior concrete barrier, ferocious dogs, minefields, the dangerous no-man's land, other obstacles and the smooth-surfaced wall itself.

In the early days, some people tried to crash through the wall with vehicles, or escape inside cars with hidden compartments. Others dug tunnels, used hot air balloons and

hang gliders, and some swam through the sewers or jumped off bridges. Maybe as many as 100 lost their lives.

In autumn 1989 communism was collapsing in Eastern Europe. At the same time, demonstrations in Leipzig against nuclear weapons and industrial pollution grew into nationwide pressure for democratic freedom. The head of the East German government was deposed. When the wall finally fell on November 9, thousands crossed to West Berlin.

In 1989 nearly two million people applied to leave, and by the end of the year 343,000 had already left. The wall had been almost totally dismantled by the end of 1990. Just a few pieces were left as a memory of a past not to be forgotten. On October 3 1990, the German flag was hoisted over the Reichstag and East and West Germany were one again.

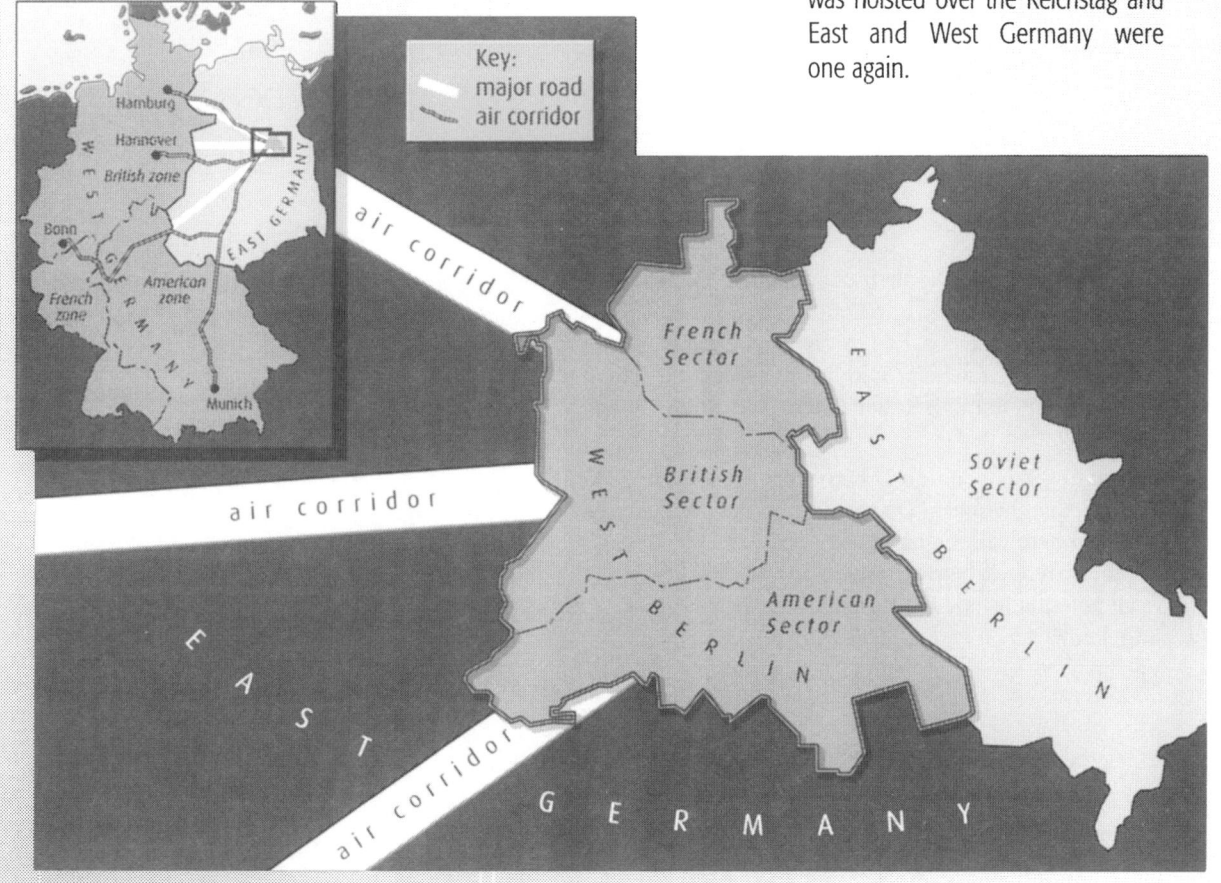

2 The good old days?

- If you haven't already done it, the listening exercise on the previous page would make a good introduction to this activity.
- This exercise is designed to explode a few myths for Western Europeans who thought life behind the Iron Curtain was one big nightmare. It should also give students in what we call ex-communist countries a chance to look back on their past and reflect on the good old days!
- Students follow the instructions on their page.

 a 2 **b** 1 **c** 5 **d** 3 **e** 4 **f** 7 **g** 6 **h** 10 **i** 9 **j** 8
1 b **2** a **3** d **4** e **5** c **6** g **7** f **8** j **9** i **10** h

- Hopefully this should lead into an interesting discussion on why, as the East German says in extract 2, you can't have paradise on earth.

Heroes' Day (not on Students' Page)

One of the first acts of the newly 'freed' socialist countries was to symbolically tear down statues of Lenin, Marx and other erstwhile 'heroes'.

A surprising number of countries have a National Heroes' Day, for example Angola, Costa Rica, Jamaica, Mozambique, Paraguay, Philippines, Sri Lanka, Uganda, Zambia and Zimbabwe. Heroes' Day has its religious equivalent in Martyrs' Day, celebrated in (amongst others) Burma, Malawi, Panama, Syria and Tunisia. Heroes' Days are virtually exclusively a third-world phenomenon. Why? In creating world empires, European countries quashed and often eradicated the traditions of the peoples they conquered. After independence these peoples went through a process of rediscovery, delving back into their own history to unearth people who symbolised in some way present expectations and aspirations. Such people could then provide a national rallying point, an emblem, a role model, and a valid alternative to western imposed ideas. Western countries, too, have their heroes, but they don't serve the same political and gut-national-feeling role as their third world counterparts.

- Ask students to discuss who their national hero is. In a monolingual class with no apparent national hero, brainstorm the class on possible contenders. Then in groups they can discuss the pros and cons of electing such people to the status of national hero. Get class feedback.
- Brainstorm to get a definition of hero. Why are there more heroes than heroines? Do we need heroes? Why do people act heroically on particular occasions? What is the difference between a hero and a celebrity? Do we all potentially have heroic qualities? What is an 'unsung' hero? etc!

2 The good old days?

Here are some extracts from interviews with people who used to live in communist (socialist) countries in Eastern Europe.

For extracts 1–5, find an extract which ...

a feels that socialism was good in principle.

b compares capitalism unfavourably with socialism.

c says propaganda in their country said a lot of true things about the West.

d regrets the fall of communism from an economic point of view.

e says propaganda in their country was negative against the West.

> **1** *Communism never existed. Only socialism. There wasn't such a gap between poor and rich people. Now everyone only thinks, 'What's best for me?' In socialist countries we were taught to think about other people. In the West everyone wants to be an individual, and in Russia we were always together, always in some group.*
>
> **(Eugenie Hupar, Russian Federation)**

> **2** *The idea was so great when the Republic began. Everybody is equal. If they had made these ideas come true, then it would have been just paradise, but you can't have paradise on earth. You can be as good as anyone else, but as soon as you get power, you just get worse and worse.*
>
> **(Eberhard Steiger, 'East' Germany)**

> **3** *We have been giving about $100 billion per year to finance the ex-DDR and to bring it up to the standards in the West. I sometimes wonder just how happy I am having to pay the so-called Solidarity Tax which helps to finance all this. Perhaps things were better when we were two separate countries.*
>
> **(Hans Luebke, West Germany)**

> **4** *I remember once watching the Olympics and I saw the sportsmen from West Germany. I thought, 'How can they look so well, because they must be so unhappy in that country?' I thought that life there was very, very bad and that almost no one had a job, that many people were lying on the streets.*
>
> **(Ina Harloff, 'East' Germany)**

> **6** *If teachers had a particular view that was different from the government, then they were not allowed to teach it. They would lose their jobs. At school we studied Russian literature and we only learned about what happened in this part of the world. It was very difficult to study English, we had to study Russian, but we could study German too. And now of course teachers have had to rewrite their history courses again.*
>
> **(Michaela Jelinkovà, Slovakia)**

> **5** *Propaganda wasn't really about how bad the West was, but about how good the East was – the fact that we had social stability and people obeyed the laws. All those things that we were told were bad in the West – crime, unemployment, beggars – have actually come true now.*
>
> **(Tamas Bartha, Hungary)**

> **7** *Before reunification only about half of West German women had a job. It wasn't like that in East Germany; nearly all the women had a job, they were equal; now only about 20% of women in the ex-DDR have jobs. In the West businessmen don't like women because they get pregnant and then the company has to pay for them.*
>
> **(Ina Harloff, 'East' Germany)**

For extracts 6–10, find an extract which ...

f regrets the fall of communism from a woman's point of view.

g says negative things about the education system under socialism.

h feels that the West was not interested in what the East had to give.

i says good and bad things about life under socialism, and that it was better then than now.

j says positive things about their education system under socialism.

> **8** *We used to have very good schools. Now there are private schools too, and these are not as good as the state schools. Before we studied all subjects, now we have to specialise when we're quite young.*
>
> **(Monika Karulová, Slovakia)**

> **9** *For normal working people socialism was great. Everyone had a job, we could all go on holiday (though only in the USSR), and we were all happy. But if you wanted to think differently, you couldn't, and you weren't allowed to read some literature and other books. But now I think the situation is much worse. Before there wasn't much difference between people; now there's an incredible gap between the very rich and the poor. There's a lot of violent crime too.*
>
> **(Janna Mesko, Russian Federation)**

> **10** *When we were unified it was like 'everything that comes from the West is right', and they took over everything. And nobody thought about making a compromise, to leave something from the Eastern part. The good things.*
>
> **(Peter Erhard, 'East' Germany)**

DAY 18 Teachers' Day

Date	varies
	October 5 (World Teachers' Day)
Level	Exs 1–3 lower intermediate
	Ex 4 upper intermediate
Age	Exs 1–3 teenagers
	Ex 4 adults
Time	Ex 1 10 minutes
	Ex 2 15 minutes
	Ex 3 15 minutes
	Ex 4 10 minutes
Vocabulary	skit, mannerism, poem, respect, experienced, compulsory, co-educational, pupil, riot, demonstration, campus, anthem, sit-in, extra-curricular

Several countries have Teachers' Days, in honour of particular teachers who were instrumental in setting the course of education in their home country. Amongst others, the Czechs commemorate Comenius' birthday (March 28), some Chinese celebrate Confucius' birthday (celebrated on different days in China and Taiwan), and the Turks remember Atatürk's death (November 24). In Argentina Teachers' Day is celebrated on September 11, and in Uruguay on September 22. In this book Teachers' Day comes chronologically in October, as in 1966 UNESCO proclaimed October 5 to be World Teachers' Day. Apparently there are more than 50 million teachers in the world – more than any other profession. And, in case you were wondering, it was George Bernard Shaw (in *Man and Superman*) who said *He who can does. He who cannot, teaches.*

1 Great teachers

- Before handing out photocopies, find out which students, if any, celebrate Teachers' Day in their country.
- Put the class into groups and ask them to describe/imagine as many ways of celebrating Teachers' Day as they can.
- Hand out photocopies and ask students to see how many of their group's ideas are mentioned in the extracts. (On page 60 you will find some information about three of the teachers mentioned in the extracts.)
- Still in groups, they discuss the answers to the questions about teachers they have known.

Follow-up

- They can then write a poem about you!
- Some time, you might like to try reversing the roles in the classroom and getting students to prepare lessons for each other, and even to write reports on teachers (which could be very, or perhaps too, revealing!).

Films

Dead Poets Society, The Prime of Miss Jean Brodie, If, Goodbye Mr Chips

2 My (ideal) English teacher is ...

- Begin with the listening activity.

Listening 1

- Students hear ten sentences about teachers. Their task is to listen and then write down as many of the sentences as they can remember.
- They can then compare their sentences with other members of their group, and see if the group as a whole can remember all ten sentences. Then play the sentences again for students to check.
- Finally, they can choose some of the sentences for discussion.

---

1 Teachers are better than books.
2 Younger teachers are generally better than older teachers.
3 Teachers cannot, and should not, be friends with their pupils.
4 Children learn more from each other than from their teachers.
5 Teachers generally don't give their pupils enough homework.
6 Primary school teachers are often better than secondary school teachers.
7 Teachers should never expose their political ideas.
8 Most teachers don't make their subjects interesting enough.
9 Strict teachers are generally the best.
10 Teachers work more than most other professions and for a lot less money.

- Students do 1–5 of the quiz – let them decide whether to answer about their ideal English teacher or about you (i.e. their English teacher).
- In pairs they then read each other's answers and decide which person (i.e. you or the ideal teacher) they were answering about. They then discuss number 6. Get class feedback!

DAY 18 Teachers' Day

1 Great teachers

a In Argentina we celebrate the death of Domingo Sarmiento who created state schools all around the country in the 1860s. Each class prepares funny skits on their teachers, imitating and exaggerating their voices and mannerisms. Then we act these out in front of the whole school.
(Deborah Longobardi, Argentina)

b March 28 is our Teachers' Day, and it is the anniversary of the birthday of Komensky. He lived in the 17th century and thought subjects should be taught together, so to teach languages, for example, he got his students to talk about world history, politics, geography – and even to sing and play sports. He was convinced that there was nothing a child couldn't do.
(Monika Karulovà, Slovakia)

c On Teachers' Day in Singapore we only have school from nine till one. Then we have parties, everybody brings food, and we draw cards for our teachers. We send flowers to the teachers we like, so if they are not popular teachers, they don't get any flowers. In Singapore our government spends a lot of money on education because they believe that we children are the future.
(Rebecca Tan Ching Kiang, Singapore)

d We dedicate our Teachers' Day to Atatürk, who was the founder of modern Turkey. The children write short poems for their teachers. I think we show much more respect to our teachers than children in the West.
(Aliye Gungor, Turkey)

e In Taiwan the schools are closed on Teachers' Day, which celebrates Confucius' birthday. The government gives prizes to the best teachers. Children send their teachers a card or flowers.
(Li-Ying Chen, Taiwan)

Think back to teachers you have had.

- Who is/was the nicest teacher?
- Which teacher are/were you most afraid of? why?
- Which teacher have you learned/did you learn the most from?
- Are/were any of your teachers unfair? Can you think of examples?
- Which teacher has had/had the greatest influence on you?

2

My (ideal) English teacher is ...

1   a   the same age as me
    b   older than me
2   a   the same sex as me
    b   the opposite sex to me
3   a   the same nationality as me
    b   a mother tongue speaker
4   a   very experienced, but not very enthusiastic
    b   very inexperienced, but very enthusiastic
5   a   someone I would like to invite for dinner
    b   someone I would never invite for dinner

6   Now put the following characteristics in order of priority.
    • sense of humour
    • ability to communicate
    • imagination
    • ability to command respect
    • understanding of students' problems
    • ability to speak students' language
    • other (you decide)

3 We don't need no education

- Hand out photocopies and tell students to choose one answer for each question in the quiz and then compare them with their partner's.

Listening 2

- Students hear some teenagers discussing the quiz. Their task is simply to identify which questions are mentioned (not all are mentioned and one is mentioned twice) and, where possible, the answers given.

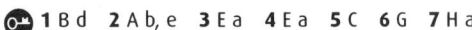 **1** B d **2** A b, e **3** E a **4** E a **5** C **6** G **7** H a

---

1 I think 18, because then, you know, you're an adult by the time you leave and you've got lots of years to learn things.

2 Well, obviously when when when you're younger you learn a lot from being at home and from your family and television and the young children's programmes.

3 I think it's up to you, isn't it? I mean everybody has totally individual tastes.

4 I definitely I think it should be up to the individual to decide what they want to do because obviously everyone wants different careers and wants to study different things.

5 Obviously there's not so many distractions if boys and girls are kept separately, but then, you know, you shouldn't really be separate, because that's just a fact of life, isn't it?

6 I really don't know. I mean I wasn't alive 20 years ago, so …

7 Now, I think they'll be the best years of your life because once you leave school, everything changes and you have so much more to worry about.

Song

- Play Pink Floyd's classic *Another Brick in the Wall* (which begins *We don't need no education*) from their album *The Wall*.

4 Students' days

- Students read the text and discuss one or more of the following questions.

1 Have you ever taken part in a sit-in or demonstration at school or university? Do these tactics usually achieve something?

2 Should all levels of education be free to everyone?

3 Should university faculties set an entrance exam or should university be open to everyone?

4 Is too much emphasis placed on exams and theory in your universities?

5 What kind of extra-curricular activities are organised at your university? Is most students' top priority to get a degree or just to enjoy themselves?

Film

Educating Rita

Here is some information about three of the teachers mentioned in Exercise 1.

John Amos Comenius (Komensky) was born in 1592 in Moravia, which is now in the Czech Republic. He believed that we are all born with a desire for knowledge and that it is the teacher's task to find the simplest and most entertaining ways of drawing out the pupils' innate capacity for learning in an atmosphere of love rather than fear. He advocated what we would now call a hands-on approach, which was radically different from the pedantic teaching methods of his time. He was particularly interested in teaching languages, which he was convinced must be learnt in the same way as the mother tongue. So his lessons revolved around topical conversations and direct contact with objects and pictures. In fact, Comenius was the first person to write illustrated books for children. Language learning was also integrated with lessons on politics, economics, world history, geography, science, the arts, handicrafts, and even singing and sports. His idea was that everything is part of something else, that no subject should be studied in isolation, and that what happened outside the classroom during playtime was just as important as what happened inside the classroom. Comenius was convinced that no expense should be spared in giving children an education and that, given the right training, there was no metaphorical mountain that could not be climbed by a child. So great has Comenius' influence been in Europe that he is now known as the Father of Modern Education. As he once said:

> The proper education of the young does not consist in stuffing their heads with a mass of words, sentences and ideas dragged together out of various authors, but in opening up their understanding to the outer world, so that a living stream may flow from their minds, just as leaves, flowers and fruit spring from the bud on a tree.

On the right to education he said:

> It is lamentable, utterly unjust and insulting that while all men are admitted to God's theatre, all are not given the chance of looking at everything. The nation is a happy one that has good schools and good books in great numbers.

The Chinese celebrate Confucius' birthday as a national holiday – Teachers' Day. This is because Confucius was the greatest of all Chinese teachers. On this day some of the most senior and the best teachers are recognised for their contribution to society. Confucius believed that everyone should be taught without any discrimination and according to their abilities. He taught his pupils/disciples (more than 3000 in his lifetime) to be self-sufficient, to be aware of their faults, and to amend them. He encouraged them not only to help themselves, but also to help others to achieve their goals. He was passionate about education:

> Learn as though you would never be able to master it; hold it as though you would be in fear of losing it.

Atatürk was the founder of modern Turkey. He gained a reputation as a great leader during military campaigns but his military prowess was really nothing compared to what he did to reform his country. In its massive scope, depth and thoroughness it compared, according to British historian Arnold Toynbee, to the Renaissance, the Reformation, the French and Industrial Revolutions all rolled into one. Atatürk believed that military victories solved little and that the true way of solving enmities between rival groups was by attaining a high level of culture. And this could only be done through education.

3

We don't need no education

A **You learn more ...**
a at school
b at home
c from your friends
d from the Internet
e from TV

C **You learn more at ...**
a same sex schools
b co-educational schools (boys and girls together)

E **Which school you go to and which subjects you study should be decided by ...**
a you
b your parents
c your teachers

G **The standard of education in your country is ...**
a better than 20 years ago
b worse than 20 years ago

B **School should be compulsory until the age of ...**
a 10   b 14
c 16   d 18

D **It's better to go to school from ...**
a 08.30 – 13.30 six days a week
b 08.30 – 15.30 five days a week

F **Exams are ...**
a a waste of time
b the only way to test pupils' learning
c an inefficient way of testing pupils' learning

H **Your school years will be/were ...**
a the best years of your life
b the worst years of your life
c somewhere in between

4

Students' days

1968 was a year of student riots around the world, particularly in France. In March that year students were arrested after anti-American demonstrations against the war in Vietnam. In May 30,000 students who had been locked out of their university campus in Paris fought the riot police with barricades, bricks, paving stones and Molotov cocktails. Throughout the summer student crowds sang the *Internationale* – the communist anthem. Students and workers in other countries joined in the protest with sit-ins, demonstrations and strikes. In Europe all this is largely forgotten, but some countries still celebrate what happened. In Senegal, fighting between the government and students in 1968 led to students getting more rights and education was assured for everyone. Every year on January 22, Students' Day, students in Senegal go into the schools to make speeches about students' position and free education. Students in Mexico also have a day when they remember that they have the right to study with the government's help.

Students rioting in the streets of Paris, 1968

DAY 19 Columbus Day

Date	October 12
Level	Ex 1 lower intermediate
	Ex 2 intermediate
Age	Ex 1 all ages
	Ex 2 mature teenagers and adults
Time	Ex 1 20 minutes
	Ex 2 15 minutes
Grammar	past simple passive
Vocabulary	maize, Incas, tobacco, print, horseshoe, sundial, gun, acorn, disease, arms, cattle, tool, sugar cane, wheat,

Columbus Day is October 12, but is celebrated in the US on the second Monday in October. Not everyone is happy about celebrating Columbus Day, in particular the native Americans who were there before Columbus arrived. Some native Americans have attributed to Columbus the Atlantic slave trade and one of the greatest waves of genocide known in history. At the time of writing a few American states celebrate either *Indigenous Peoples' Day* or *Native American Day,* as a rival festival to Columbus Day.

For information about the flat earth theory, see page 107.

1 History quiz

- Before handing out photocopies, ask the whole class this simple question: Who discovered America? Apart from the fact that Indians were already there, try to elicit Columbus. (Some students may mention Leif Ericson, the Viking explorer who reached Newfoundland in the 11th century, and who has his own day on October 9.) Here are a few questions to test students' knowledge of Columbus:

1 Where and approximately when was Columbus born?

2 Which Queen gave Columbus her patronage?

3 Why did Columbus decide to travel west? Where did he think he was when he arrived?

4 When did Columbus arrive in America?

1 In Italy, in 1452.

2 Queen Isabel of Spain

3 To find a new route to the Far East. He thought he was on the east coast of India, which is why he called the natives Indians.

4 In 1492.

- Now hand out photocopies. Ask students to look at the picture of a modern kitchen and to put a tick in the box against items they think might have been around in Columbus' time. This should entail a group discussion on when the various items were discovered/invented. The word for 'potato' varies wonderfully from language to language; check this out with your students.

Listening
- Students listen and check if they were right.

Only the newspaper was not in use in Columbus' time.

1 Maize was 'discovered' by Columbus, but was introduced to Europe by Cortés.

2 Potatoes were originally cultivated by the Incas and were discovered in Peru by Pizzarro who brought them to Europe in 1534. The English naval man, Sir Walter Raleigh discovered them in Virginia 50 years after Pizzarro.

3 Rubber was only used on a large scale in Europe in the 19th century. The earliest reference to rubber by a European was in 1530 to describe an Aztec ball game.

4 Haitian Indians used to roll dried tobacco leaves into a pipe. A variation of this habit was introduced into Europe by the Spanish in the early 16th century.

5 The first book to be printed was in Korea in 704. Europe had to wait until 1451. Paper money was printed in Persia in 1014.

6 The first horseshoes were made in around 900.

7 Coffee was first domesticated in north-east Africa, and was already being drunk over 2000 years ago.

8 Some of the first clocks were the sundials used by the ancient Egyptians, and the water clocks by the Greeks and Romans. The first mechanical clock in Europe was produced in 1283.

9 The Chinese were the first to use guns in 1128. The first in Europe were the Italians in 1326.

Films
Christopher Columbus (1949), *Christopher Columbus – The Discovery* (1992), which just beat *1492 – Conquest of Paradise* to the big screen. If you can get hold of more than one of these films, why not choose a similar scene and see how the two producers approach it.

2 Americans

- Students read the text and answer the questions.

The quotation is loosely based on the words of Powhatan, Chief of the Powhatan Confederacy, which although said in 1609 (over 100 years after Columbus' departure), are very relevant to how the native Indians got treated by the white settlers.

- If students have studied a bit of history, they could also discuss the general mentality in Europe from the time of Columbus through to the 20th century, and how it compares with attitudes to ethnic minorities, and American Indians in particular, today.

DAY 19 Columbus Day

1 History quiz

2 Americans

Don't you understand that I don't want to be your enemy? Do you really think I prefer lying cold in the woods instead of sleeping quietly with my wives and children? I would much prefer eating good meat with you than eating acorns and roots in the wood. I want to laugh with you, not be hunted by you. Let us be friends then. Do not invade us with such an armed force. Lay aside these arms.

1 Who do you think spoke these words? What would your reply have been?

2 What do you know about Indians in America (both North and South)? How did they live before the white man came? And now?

3 Here is a list of things that Europeans brought to America. Put them in order of utility.
Christianity   diseases   guns   horses and cattle   ideas and philosophies
iron tools   new kinds of plants   new technologies   Roman law
sugar cane and wheat

4 Would the world be a better place if America had never been discovered?

5 How are ethnic minorities treated in your country, and what rights should these minorities be given?

DAY 20 United Nations' Day

Date	October 24
Level	intermediate
Age	all ages
Time	Ex 1 20 minutes
	Ex 2 15 minutes
Vocabulary	charter, war, vote, army, troops, personnel, peace-keeping force, refugee, agency, campaign, employee, budget, allocation, land mine, counter, foster, nutrition, relief, proceedings, tribunal

UN Day is celebrated on 24 October but this lesson could obviously be used at any time when the UN is headline news. Most of us know surprisingly little about the world's peace-keeping force, but this should be a reason *for* doing this lesson, not *against* it. Unlike most of the other material in this book, some of the information here is likely to date. So it would be a good idea if you could find out some of the UN's more recent activities, especially if you intend brainstorming your class on the role of the UN today. The best way to get information on the UN is off the Internet.

The biggest contributors to the UN are: US, Japan, Germany, France, UK, Italy, Russia.

1 United Nations – facts and figures

- Before handing out photocopies, write the following quotation on the board: 'A business with 185 members on the board, all of them with strong and contradictory opinions, coming from every conceivable culture, speaking every conceivable language – and each with a brother-in-law who is unemployed.' Ask students to guess what business is being described.

- It was an American ambassador's description of the United Nations.

- Ask students if they know when and why the UN was founded and whether their country is a member or not.

- Hand out photocopies. In groups students see if they can make educated guesses for some of the numbers.

Listening

- Students' task is to listen and correct the figures they wrote on the text.

- **1** 1945 **2** 10 **3** 55 **4** 1950 **5** 40 **6** 30 **7** 1300 **8** 80 **9** 70 **10** 51,000

On 25th June 1945, 51 countries met in San Francisco to sign the Charter of the United Nations. Their main aim was to make sure that never again so many lives would be lost in war. In fact, around ten million soldiers had died in the First World War and 55 million in the Second. The original 51 members have now become 185 and each state has one vote, no matter how small they are.

The UN doesn't have its own army. Instead, member states voluntarily supply troops and personnel. The first peace-keeping force was used in 1950, during the crisis in Korea. Since then the UN has been involved in about 40 peace missions, and has helped more than 30 million refugees. About 1300 UN peacekeepers have died on duty. Less than 3% were Americans.

But keeping the peace is only a small part of the United Nations' work. About 80% of their effort is devoted to helping countries to learn how to help themselves. For instance the UN agency responsible for education, science and culture is called UNESCO. It has led a campaign to help people in poorer countries to read and write. In 1970 only 10 per cent of Ethiopians could read and write. Now the figure is over 70 per cent.

Originally only 1500 people worked for the UN. Now there are 51,000 employees all around the world.

2 Budget allocation

- Students imagine they are having a meeting of the General Assembly of the United Nations. They have to decide how to allocate the annual budget. (In reality the UN's total budget, including money for related agencies, would be around $20 billion.) Students decide what percentage of the total budget they would allocate to each of the areas listed.

- This exercise is designed to showcase some of the other activities that the UN does that often get shrouded by the UN's much publicised military role. This is basically a prioritising exercise, but in some sense it is a realistic simulation of the kind of decision-making that top-level UN officials have to make. Obviously it would be nice to get hold of some real statistics on how much money is allocated to the various activities, but I haven't been able to find such data.

DAY 20 United Nations' Day

1 United Nations – facts and figures

On 25th June (1)———— , 51 countries met in San Francisco to sign the Charter of the United Nations. Their main aim was to make sure that never again so many lives would be lost in war. In fact, around (2)———— million soldiers had died in the First World War and (3)———— million in the Second. The original 51 members have now become 185 and each state has one vote, no matter how small they are.

The UN doesn't have its own army. Instead, member states voluntarily supply troops and personnel. The first peace-keeping force was used in (4)———— , during the crisis in Korea. Since then the UN has been involved in about (5)———— peace missions, and has helped more than (6)———— million refugees. About (7)———— UN peacekeepers have died on duty. Less than 3% were Americans.

But keeping the peace is only a small part of the United Nations' work. About (8)———— per cent of their effort is devoted to helping countries to learn how to help themselves. For instance the UN agency responsible for education, science and culture is called UNESCO. It has led a campaign to help people in poorer countries to read and write. In 1970 only 10 per cent of Ethiopians could read and write. Now the figure is over (9)———— per cent.

Originally only 1500 people worked for the UN. Now there are (10)———— employees all around the world.

2 Budget allocation

- 🗡 Assisting countries devastated by war and long-term threat of land mines
- 🗡 Banning nuclear weapons from outer space
- 🗡 Bringing an end to colonialism
- 🗡 Countering global crime and drug trafficking
- 🗡 Fostering world cooperation in better housing, family planning and crime prevention
- 🗡 Helping children through immunisation, primary health care, nutrition and basic education
- 🗡 Providing relief assistance to refugees and disaster victims
- 🗡 Recommending measures to reduce the gap between rich and poor countries
- 🗡 Peace keeping
- 🗡 Promoting and protecting democracy and human rights
- 🗡 Monitoring elections
- 🗡 Saving children from starvation and disease
- 🗡 Spreading the benefits of science and technology
- 🗡 Starting proceedings against war criminals, through international tribunals

DAY 21 Halloween

Date	October 31
Level	intermediate
Age	all ages, especially teenagers
Time	Ex 1 20 minutes
	Ex 2 15 minutes
	Ex 3 10 minutes
Vocabulary	feast, the dead, magical, the living, burial mound, torch, bonfire, ancestor, spirit, soul, trick, practical joke, treat, turnip, pumpkin, hollow out, carve, witch, candy, toilet paper, flour, spooky, duck (v), peel, poltergeist, faith healer, lucky charm, witch doctor

Halloween is celebrated on October 31 in both Britain and (with a little more fervour) in the US. The word Halloween derives from All Hallows' Eve. Hallow means 'saint' and, in fact, November 1 in the Christian calendar is All Saints' Day. The eve of Hallowmass was recognised as an official Christian festival by the Pope in 1006.

Before the Christians came along it had been a Celtic festival called Samhain. The Celts were not alone in celebrating this day as a feast of the dead; apparently the Egyptians had done so before them, and the Aztecs after them. Nor is 'trick or treating' an exclusively Celtic tradition. On the eve of the last Wednesday of the Persian year, known as Red Wednesday's Eve, modern Iranians still leap through bonfire flames, run down streets banging on pots and pans and knock on doors asking for treats.

Halloween began to be celebrated in the US at the time of the mass emigration of the Irish during the potato famine.

1 Past and present

- Before handing out photocopies, ask students if they know in which country Halloween originated (most will say America, but don't say anything at this point) and how old the festival is.

- Then ask them if they know any of the related customs – again don't tell them if they are right or wrong.

- Hand out photocopies and ask students to look at the illustrations (but not read the texts) and decide which ones refer to the way Halloween is celebrated now and which refer to how it used to be celebrated in the past.

- Then students should match the illustrations with the texts below and they will be able to see how right or wrong they were in relation to the origins and customs of Halloween.

Pictures 1, 4 and 5 refer to the past, pictures 2 and 3 to the present.

  1 c   2 e   3 d   4 b   5 a

DAY 21 Halloween

1 Past and present

1

2

3

4

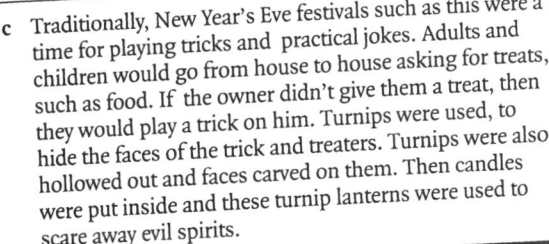

5

a The Celts were the first to celebrate October 31, which was their feast of the dead, known as Samhain. Samhain meant 'end of the summer' and coincided with the beginning of the Celtic year. The change from one year to another was a magical time, and the Celts believed that on this night the dead could come back and communicate with the living. In fact in Ireland they used to open up the great burial mounds and line the walls with lighted torches so that the dead could find their way out.

b The Celts also used to light great bonfires. A special feast was prepared and a place left for an unseen visitor – perhaps the Great Mother, who was the original ancestor of the tribe. The spirits of the dead would appear in the smoke of the bonfire, and also the souls of children who were about to be born.

c Traditionally, New Year's Eve festivals such as this were a time for playing tricks and practical jokes. Adults and children would go from house to house asking for treats, such as food. If the owner didn't give them a treat, then they would play a trick on him. Turnips were used, to hide the faces of the trick and treaters. Turnips were also hollowed out and faces carved on them. Then candles were put inside and these turnip lanterns were used to scare away evil spirits.

d The Samhain custom of 'trick or treat' still survives today. In both the US and the UK children wearing masks knock on people's doors asking for candies/sweets (treats). If people refuse to give the children anything, then the children play some practical joke on them (trick), such as removing gates, whitewashing over house windows, hiding animals, etc. Turnip lanterns have nowadays been replaced by pumpkin lanterns, especially in the United States.

e When Christianity became strong, the Church tried to suppress the pagan festival of Samhain by replacing it with a Christian festival of the dead. In this case only the saintly dead were remembered, and it became known as All Hallows' (saints/souls) Eve. But there are still some witches, Wiccans, who observe Halloween as a religious festival. Whole families, or covens, as witch families are known, come together to exchange ideas and to celebrate their Feast of Life in Death.

2 Halloween celebrations

- Hand out photocopies. Students who do celebrate Halloween can fill in the table. Those who don't can move straight on to the listening.

Listening

- Students listen and fill in the first two columns of the table. Make sure they understand that one girl is American (Speaker B) and the other is English (Speaker C).

	US	UK
Costumes	✔	?
Treats:		
money	✗	✔
candy/sweets	✔	✔
Tricks:		
toilet paper in trees	✔	✗
flour	?	✔
Pumpkin lantern	✔	✔

A And since we're on the subject of Halloween, Clare, tell me, what ... how do the Americans celebrate Halloween? Is it ...

B Oh, it's great. It's the best holiday. You go and you dress up in whatever kind of costume you want to, anything from a ghost to, I don't know, someone from *Star Wars* if you want to. And then you run around to people's houses and you ask them for money. Money? No. For candy. Sorry. No, I don't know anyone who asks for money, no, you definitely ask for candy. And you say 'Trick or treat?', which you probably know about.

A Trick, trick or treat.

C Yes, because it's the same here. [yeah, yeah] We do the same thing.

A But do they do they ask for money here? I mean sweets.

C They ask for sweets, but a lot of people don't have treats to give them, so sometimes they feel guilty and so they give them money instead of nothing.

B Oh, maybe that's where I got the money thing from.

A Right, right, no well that sounds ...

B Oh and and the trick is often, they put for some reason, you take toilet paper and you put it all in the trees in their garden. Very obnoxious, [Really?] it's very hard to get out.

C We're not, we're not so bold over here. I don't think we do such bad things. If you get something really bad, it's like having flour chucked at your front door or something, really, not so bad like that.

A That's really nice. And what about the pumpkin phenomenon? [Oh, yes] Do they have ... they cut these pumpkins up in a kind of way?

B Do they do that here? [Do they do ...?]

C Yeah [that's great] I still do that now.

B Do you? You get the pumpkin, and then you carve out the inside and you make a face.

C You put it in your window [yeah, like a lantern] so then at night you can all see all the pumpkins with candles in the windows.

A Spooky.

B Nice though. Fun.

3 The supernatural

- Students read the text and then discuss the list in groups.

Follow-up

- You could continue the theme of good and bad luck by asking students, in pairs, to jot down three things which are considered lucky in their country and three which are unlucky, e.g. black cats, walking under a ladder, four-leaved clovers, etc. Then have a class discussion to find out how many things they wrote in common.

2 Halloween celebrations

Do you celebrate Halloween?
If so, fill in the last column
of the table.

	US	UK	You
Do you dress up in costumes?			
What kind of treats do you receive?			
– money?			
– candy/sweets?			
– other?			
What kind of tricks do you play?			
– hang toilet paper in trees?			
– throw flour at people's front doors?			
– other?			
Do you make a lantern with a pumpkin?			

3 The supernatural

Traditionally Samhain was a time of fortune telling.
Marriages were foretold by ducking for apples in water. The
first person to bite an apple would be the first to marry.
Then by peeling an apple you could see how long your life
would be; for example, if you managed one long peel you
would have a very long life.

Do you have fortune tellers in your country? Do people in
your country believe in any of the people and things below?

 ghosts

 fairies

 voodoo

 poltergeists

 the evil eye

 faith healers

 lucky charms

 witch doctors/shamans

 bearers of good/bad luck

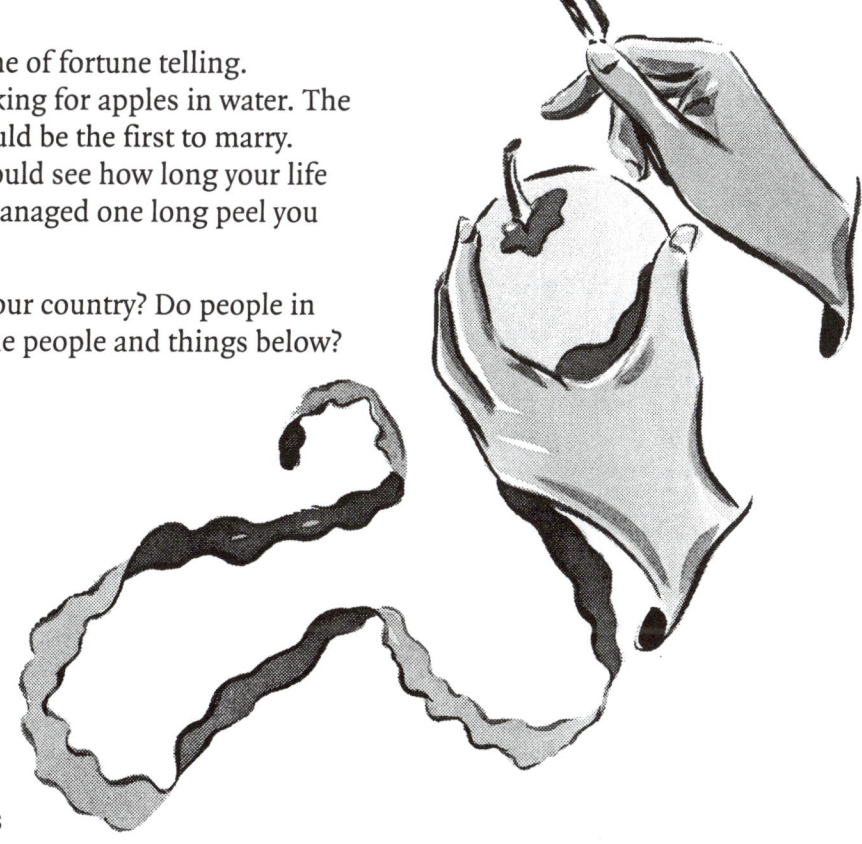

DAY 22 Day of the Dead

Date	November 2 (Christian)
	other religions may vary
Level	upper intermediate
Age	all ages
Time	Ex 1 15 minutes
	Ex 2 15 minutes
Advice	Death may be a difficult subject for some students to talk about.
Vocabulary	sin, sinner, hell, heaven, purgatory, skull, skeleton, grave, ancestor, pray, ghost, monk, health, idol worship, ritual

Most countries have a day on which they remember the dead. For the Christian church this is traditionally on November 2 (All Souls' Day), though in Armenia, for instance, it is celebrated on Easter Monday. Beliefs in where the dead go, especially evil people, is a fascinating subject. In ancient mythology Hell was more like Purgatory, and was the underground place where everyone went before being judged. Hades, where the souls of the dead were taken across the river Styx, was originally a person not a place. He was the son of Kronos and brother of Zeus and Poseidon.

1 Remembering the dead

- Get students to write down a few sentences on how they imagine Hell and Heaven (or their equivalents) to be. Then in groups students compare their ideas.
- Hand out photocopies and ask students to read the text and then answer the questions.

2 Songs for our ancestors

- On page 108 you will find four poems connected with ancestors. Photocopy these and hand them out.

Listening

- Students hear the poems on their page. They are extracts from poems written by natives of colonised countries who remember their ancestors and (apart from the first poem) the way things used to be before the white man came. I had thought about blanking out some of the words in the poems for students to fill in as they were listening, but I think this would destroy the beauty and simplicity of these poems. I wouldn't play them one after another, but individually. For the first poem, only the Acholi version, not the English, has been recorded (you could also play the recording before handing out the photocopies and get students to guess what language it is, or at least from which continent it comes). The task should simply be to enjoy the poems and to discuss their meaning and the poets' reasons for writing them. Students can also discuss which one they like best and why, including a discussion on rhyme, layout of the poem, etc.

Follow-up

- Students discuss to what extent they think they have been moulded by their nation's past, and whether they are proud of that past. This could lead on to a discussion on ethnic groups, white man's follies, and racism in general.

1

Remembering the dead

Christians believed that people who committed major crimes or sins went straight to Hell when they died, where they burned forever. Minor sinners went to Purgatory, where they had to suffer for their sins before going to Heaven. Belgians used to say, 'The more cakes you eat on this night, the more souls you can save from Purgatory.' Catholics in many countries make special food for the dead in the form of skulls, bones, skeletons or even coffins. This food is then left on the grave or members of the family have a picnic near the grave and sing and talk about their dead relatives. In Hungary people believe that if you don't go to the cemetery, your dead relatives' ghosts will come to your house, and in parts of Sicily (Italy) it is believed that the dead come to houses to give children presents.

In many parts of Africa, ancestors are considered to be important members of the family, in the same way as living relatives. In Uganda ancestors are buried near the houses and Acholi people go to them to pray before hunting or harvesting, or if there is a problem in the family. Some Central Africans carry bags of fetishes, little figures that represent their ancestors, and these are believed to have magic powers such as curing diseases. The Ashanti in Ghana have special ceremonies known as *Adae Kese*. Stools represent the ancestors and food and drink are placed in front of them. The ancestors are asked to speak to the gods for them and to give them health and good fortune.

At the Japanese festival of *Obon*, 27 lanterns are lit to guide the spirits of the ancestors on their annual visit to the family home. One ancient festival in China was called *Time of Sending Winter Clothes to Ancestors*. Suits of winter clothes were cut out of paper and addressed personally to the ancestors. These were then burned and it was believed that the ancestors would be warmly clothed. In China still today people try to ensure that their dead relatives will go to the other world, even those who have done bad in their lives, by paying monks to pray for these relatives. In Korea, one traditional ceremony for honouring the dead, known as *che-sa*, is forbidden by the Christian church as it breaks the commandments against idol worship and worship of other gods.

Australian aborigines used to cut up their dead relatives into pieces and carry them round in bags for eating later. The idea was that the spirit and wisdom of the dead relative would enter the body of the living.

1 How do you celebrate your dead? Which of the customs described above is most similar to your customs? What do you think of the other customs?

2 How much is death talked about in your society?

3 What rituals are associated with death in your country?

4 What do you believe happens after we die?

DAY 23 Guy Fawkes' Night

Date	November 5
Level	upper intermediate
Age	all ages, especially teenagers
Time	20 minutes
Vocabulary	gunpowder, plot, Protestant, Catholic, depose, law, service, confiscate, traitor, fanatical, Houses of Parliament, conspirator, anonymous letter, tunnel (v), search party, penny for the guy, fireworks, effigy, bonfire, barrel, cellar

November 5 is celebrated in England as Guy Fawkes' Night. It is named after a member of a group of Catholic conspirators who, in 1605, plotted to blow up the English Houses of Parliament with gunpowder. The conspirators were arrested, hanged, drawn and quartered and then, so legend has it, thrown on a bonfire. Whilst November 5 celebrates a relatively important historical event (the exact details of which few adults can probably remember!), the main attraction is really the bonfire and fireworks display, which is something nearly all cultures have.

Bonfires have been lit around this time since Celtic times. At this time of year the sun is getting weaker and the Celts thought that bonfires might give it a bit of extra strength.

Guy Fawkes is not the only person to get his effigy burnt on November 5. Mary I, the queen before Elizabeth I, ordered 17 Protestant martyrs to be burnt at Lewes in Sussex, where every November 5 they burn an effigy of the Pope.

Many bonfire celebrations in England used to end up in riots between the police and the bonfire boys, the gangs in charge.

Children in Britain today go around with an effigy of Guy Fawkes and collect money (to buy fireworks with) crying 'penny for the guy'. On the night itself people light enormous bonfires and set off fireworks. These events take place either in private gardens or public parks. The injuries as a result of fireworks can sometimes be fatal – two children died in 1994, a year in which a record 1574 people needed hospital treatment. More recent years have seen a decline in numbers, and many people campaign against the fact that children can buy fireworks, that they cause a lot of noise and nuisance, and that animals, too, get injured.

Other countries have their own fireworks and lantern festivals. For centuries the Chinese set off fireworks at their festivities. When trade between the East and West began, the Chinese became major producers of fireworks. In Italy they were manufactured in the early 16th century, and the French and the English began using them too. Most of our most popular modern fireworks – rockets, bombs and catherine wheels, were commonly used at this time.

The propelling and exploding force in fireworks comes from a combination of saltpetre, sulphur and charcoal. The scientific word for fireworks is 'pyrotechnics' from the Greek meaning 'fire arts', and in fact fireworks preceded guns.

The Gunpowder Plot

- Students read the brief background story to the Gunpowder Plot as a preview to the listening exercise.

Listening

- Students hear a jumbled (and extremely potted) version of the story of Guy Fawkes. Their task is to match each piece with the relevant illustration, which is already in order. Good students could then write the story out.

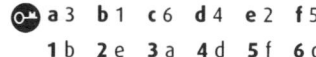 **a** 3 **b** 1 **c** 6 **d** 4 **e** 2 **f** 5
1 b **2** e **3** a **4** d **5** f **6** c

1 At that time the Houses of Parliament had two floors. The Lords met on the upper floor, below were some old kitchens. In May 1604 one of the conspirators managed to rent the house next door to the kitchen area. In December they began tunnelling from the house into the parliament buildings. The stone was very thick and they made little progress.

2 Guy Fawkes was found and the search party uncovered the gunpowder under a pile of wood. Fawkes was arrested, and later the rest of the conspirators too. They were hung, drawn and quartered and their bodies were thrown onto bonfires. November 5 was then officially celebrated as a day of thanksgiving for 250 years.

3 In 1604 Robert Catesby decided that assassinating James I was not enough. The whole Protestant government needed to be eliminated. He discussed his plans with five other Catholic conspirators, including a certain Guido Fawkes, in an old lodging house, near an inn.

4 The conspirators waited for the opening of a new parliament. But one of them realised that the massive explosion might kill some ex-Catholic lords who had been forced to become Protestants. So an anonymous letter was sent to one of these lords warning him of the plot. The letter was given to the prime minister, who ordered a search to be made.

5 Today, children in Britain go around begging for a penny for the guy to buy money for fireworks. They then build enormous bonfires, burn effigies of Guy Fawkes, and watch fantastic firework displays.

6 While they were tunnelling one day, Guy Fawkes discovered that coal was being removed from a cellar directly under where many of the lords often sat. The conspirators quickly transferred 36 barrels of gunpowder into the cellar.

- When students have checked their answers, let them hear the second part of the recording – the story in the correct order.

The Gunpowder Plot

Elizabeth I made England one of Europe's strongest Protestant nations and was consequently formally deposed as Head of the Church of England by the Pope in 1570. Catholic Spain tried to invade England in 1588 but failed. The result was a series of severe anti-Catholic laws: Catholic church services were forbidden, and any man who didn't attend the Anglican Church was fined £20 and might have his land confiscated. Catholics in England were seen as traitors. When James I came to the throne in 1603 he relaxed the anti-Catholic laws and Catholics began to show their power again. James panicked. He ordered all Catholic priests out of the country and brought back the anti-Catholic laws. To a fanatical young Catholic called Robert Catesby, the only solution seemed to be violence.

DAY 24 Remembrance Day

Date	November 11
Level	Exs 1 and 2 intermediate
	Exs 3 and 4 upper intermediate
Ages	all ages
Time	Ex 1 15 minutes
	Ex 2 15 minutes
	Ex 3 15 minutes
	Ex 4 20 minutes
Vocabulary	armistice, veteran, poppy, amputee, flag, service, wreath, Unknown Warrior, army, retirement, pride, challenge, sleep deprivation, combat arms, private (n), jail, land mines, culture shock, infantry

Remembrance Day (November 11) commemorates the signing of the armistice at the end of the First World War. In France it is still known as Armistice Day. Americans also celebrate Memorial Day (on May 30 or the last Monday of May) and Veterans' Day. 'Armistice' means a truce preliminary to signing a peace treaty: a veteran is an old experienced soldier.

1 'Greater love ...'

• Begin with the listening exercise.

Listening 1

• Students hear the origin of Remembrance Day. Dictate the following questions:

1 At what time, day, month and year was the First World War armistice signed?

2 In Britain and Canada what is Armistice Day known as?

3 For who is money collected?

4 Which famous person attends the ceremony in Whitehall, London?

5 How long is the period of silence?

6 Who does the Unknown Warrior represent?

7 When did Eisenhower change the name to Veterans' Day?

 1 11 am on 11.11.1918

   2 Remembrance Day.

   3 War veterans and amputees.

   4 The Queen.

   5 Two minutes.

   6 All who died.

   7 In 1954.

November 11 was first proclaimed Armistice Day in 1919, to celebrate the signing in 1918 at 11.00 am on the 11th day of the 11th month of the armistice that brought the First World War to an end. It then changed its name to Remembrance Day in Britain and Canada, where people raise money by selling poppies to help war veterans and amputees.

In France the President of the Republic makes a speech on television and the veterans make little sticks with the French flag to sell in the streets. The French also celebrate May the eighth, which was the last day of the Second World War.

In Britain, on the second Sunday of November, various services are held throughout the country, the most important being at the Cenotaph in Whitehall, London. The services include a two-minute silence. The King or Queen places a wreath on the tomb of the Unknown Warrior, who is a representative of all who died.

In the United States, Armistice Day was observed until 1954, when President Eisenhower signed an act of Congress 'to honor veterans on the eleventh day of November each year ... a day dedicated to world peace', and since then in the US the day has been known as Veterans' Day.

• Again before handing out photocopies, ask students what they know about major wars since 1945. Get them to estimate how many people they think have been killed in war since the end of the Second World War, and ask for a few guesses about the number of fatalities in particular wars. Then ask them to list the five countries with the biggest armies in the world.

• Then hand out the photocopies and students can check their answers with the tables.

The top five exporters of major arms are: Russia, USA, France, UK, China. Spending $1 billion on guided missile production creates 9000 jobs; the same money would create 63,000 jobs in education. The biggest military spenders are Iraq, Israel, Oman and Saudi Arabia. Nine out of ten victims of war are civilians. 80% of refugees are women and children.

2 War

• In October 1963, Ethiopia's Emperor, Haile Selassie (Ras Tafari Makonnen) made a speech about racial discrimination to the United Nations. His words became the basis for Bob Marley's song *War* (from his *Exodus* album). If you have access to a recording of this song, you could black out some of the words and make it into a listening comprehension exercise. This song also has the advantage of being sung slowly, so students should be able to follow without problems.

• If you don't have access to a recording, students can simply read the words and debate what stands in the way of this day ever arriving.

DAY 24 Remembrance Day

1 'Greater love ...'

Greater love hath no man than this, that a man lay down his life for his friends.

John 15 v. 13

	People killed in wars
WW1	10 million
WW2	55 million (20 million in USSR)
Korea	2 million
Cambodia	1 million
Vietnam	2 million
Biafra-Nigeria	1 million
Iran/Iraq	1 million
Total since 1945	**about 20 million**

Largest armed forces active today *in millions*
China 2.9
USA 1.5
India 1.3
Russia 1.2
N. Korea 0.8

2 War

Until the philosophy which holds one race
Superior and another inferior
Is finally and permanently discredited and abandoned
Everywhere is war, me say war

That until there are no longer first class
And second class citizens of any nation
Until the colour of a man's skin
Is of no more significance than the colour of his eyes
Me say war

That until the basic human rights are equally
Guaranteed to all, without regard to race
Dis a war

That until that day
The dream of lasting peace, world citizenship
Rule of international morality
Will remain in but a fleeting illusion
To be pursued, but never attained
Now everywhere is war, war

And until the ignoble and unhappy regimes
That hold our brothers in Angola, in Mozambique,
South Africa sub-human bondage
Have been toppled, utterly destroyed
Well, everywhere is war, me say war

War in the east, war in the west
War up north, war down south
War, war, rumours of war

And until that day, the African continent
Will not know peace, we Africans will fight

We find it necessary and we know we shall win
As we are confident in the victory

Of good over evil, good over evil, good over evil
Good over evil, good over evil, good over evil

Haile Selassie/Bob Marley

3 Why join the army?

- Before students look at the exercise, brainstorm on reasons for and against joining the army. Then get them to see which reasons are mentioned on their page.

Listening 2

- A Welsh and an American officer talk about army life. Students match each listening extract with the pros and cons on their page (not all of which are mentioned in the recording).

 **1** b, e **2** j, c **3** g **4** d **5** k **6** i **7** h

1 There's early retirements for fifteen years – there's very few other things that you could work at just for fifteen years and be able to retire. And just, you know, the pride of serving, somebody's got to do it. Where would any country be without some type of military force? [Right] And most people that do that take pride in serving their country.

2 What some people would consider bad are part of what some people would consider the challenge, such as sleep deprivation. When you're working in the field you get very tired, at times, especially during combat arms, you don't have regular sleep or regular food, there's a lot of pressure.

3 With the Uniform Code of Military Justice and the authority that that gives commanders to uh direct you to do things whether you want to do them or not. You're educated as a private on what the consequences will be if you choose not to follow an order. Usually in time of peace you can go to jail for a considerable amount of time. In time of war you could be shot.

4 Well the majority of people are attracted by the adventure, travel and the challenge. And we do have a lot of people who join because of the family connection, fathers, brothers, uncles, even grandfathers who've been in the services.

5 And when you go from from that type of a life twenty-four hours seven day a week with the threat of land mines or being shot at, always being on your toes kind of thing, and then go back to your regular home life, there's ... it's a culture shock.

6 They're not allowed at present to join what we call combat arms, which is infantry, the Royal Armour Corps and some branches of the Royal Engineers, because of the type of work that they're expected to do. It's not considered morally correct in Britain at present for them to be directly involved in war. Though the Israeli army and the Danish army are both doing it.

7 You spend a lot of time away from your families and occasionally you have language problems.

4 Conscious

- Ask students to read the poem *Conscious* and then ask the whole class where they think the man is and what has happened to him. Develop this into a discussion of the effects of war on soldiers during the following stages: when they are called up for service, when they are on their way to the battlefield, when they are actually at the battlefield, when they are wounded, when the war ends, ten years after the war has ended.

- Then ask them to read the poem in more detail, thinking about some of the following points.
  1 why his fingers wake first
  2 what 'flutter' might mean
  3 what connection there is between his eyes and the blinds
  4 what the may-flowers represent
  5 how a sense of panic and paranoia is created
  6 how his senses have become muddled
  7 how the poet blends the narrator's and the soldier's voices together
  8 how and why the poet refrains from making a direct comment on the horrors of war
  9 whether the ending is successful
  10 the meaning of the title

- Now get them to try reading the poem aloud, trying to make it as dramatic as possible.

Listening 3

- Finally they can listen to the recorded version and see if it coincides with their interpretation of how the poem should be read.

3 Why join the army?

Which of the following do you think are good reasons for joining the army?

a The army pays for your college/university education.

b You can retire with a pension after (15) years' service.

c Because you would enjoy being part of combat action.

d For the travel.

e For the pride of serving your country.

f For companionship.

Which do you think are the worst aspects of army life?

g Being ordered to do what you don't want to do.

h Being away from your family.

i (for men) The fact that there are no women in some branches of the army.

j Sleep deprivation.

k Fear of being killed.

"YOUR COUNTRY NEEDS YOU"

4 Conscious

His fingers wake, and flutter; up the bed,
His eyes come open with a pull of will,
Helped by the yellow may-flowers by his head.
The blind-cord drawls across the window-sill ...
What a smooth floor the ward has! What a rug!
Who is that talking out of sight?
Why are they laughing? What's inside that jug?
"Nurse! Doctor!" – " Yes; all right, all right."

But sudden evening muddles all the air –
There seems to be no time to want a drink of water,
Nurse looks so far away. And here and there
Music and roses burst through crimson slaughter.
He can't remember where he saw blue sky.
More blankets. Cold. He's cold. And yet so hot.
And there's no light to see the voices by;
There is not time to ask – he knows not what.

Wilfred Owen

DAY 25 Thanksgiving

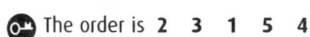 The order is **2 3 1 5 4**

Date	4th Thursday in November (US)
Level	Ex 1 intermediate
	Exs 2 and 3 upper intermediate
Age	all ages
Time	Ex 1 15 minutes
	Ex 2 10 minutes
	Ex 3 15 minutes
Advice	Exs 2 and 3 are political.
Vocabulary	Protestant, Puritan, Catholic, found (v), Netherlands, pioneer, Pilgrim, settler, harvest, feast, Indian, seeds, turkey, corn, hunt, myth, indigenous, ban, myth, distort, romanticise, conflict, melting pot, holy kingdom, Satan, torture, genocide, plague, smallpox, exterminate, refugee, slave trade

In the USA this is celebrated on the fourth Thursday in November, making a long weekend through to Monday. It is one of America's most important holidays, and a time when families reunite for a big Thanksgiving dinner.

Thanksgiving became a national holiday due to the author of the nursery rhyme 'Mary had a little lamb', Sarah Josepha Hale, who began her campaign in 1846. George Washington had proclaimed a national Thanksgiving day to honour the new Constitution, and Hale proposed calling it Union Thanksgiving, as she hoped the states would thus be brought into closer union. Anyway, she won the support of Lincoln, who chose 6 August as the date, though the following year Thanksgiving was proclaimed a national holiday on the last Thursday of November. But Roosevelt felt that it was a bit too close to Christmas, so in 1939 Thanksgiving was held on the third Thursday. Finally, in 1941, a joint resolution in Congress established it once and for all on the fourth Thursday.

This unit has two very different listening exercises. The first, for low levels, takes the Thanksgiving story literally. The second, for higher levels, explodes the myth. However, unless your higher level students are already familiar with the traditional Thanksgiving story, you may like to run through exercise 1 with them first.

1 The Mayflower

- Brainstorm to see if students know anything about the Pilgrim Fathers. Then hand out photocopies and ask them to read the text for a little background history before listening to the traditionally given origins of the Thanksgiving festival.

Listening 1

- Students first hear the story of Thanksgiving in the wrong order. Pause after each section for them to write a very brief summary of each point. In pairs, they then compare their summaries and decide what order the five pieces should be in.

- They then listen again, this time to a continuous piece in the correct sequence.

1 Fortunately the first year's harvest was good. The Pilgrims wanted to thank both God and also the Indians. So the governor declared a feast and invited the Indians to join in. About ninety Indians brought along fish, deer meat, turkey and pumpkin. The Indians taught the Pilgrims how to crush corn and make it into hot corn-meal bread. They feasted with the English settlers for three days.

2 In 1620 a group of English people who were unhappy with the way the Church of England was organised set sail from Plymouth on a ship called the Mayflower. They wanted to found a new church in America.

3 After six weeks at sea, the Pilgrims landed at what is now Plymouth Rock, Massachusetts, in 1620. They had a hard winter and nearly half of them died. But the local Indians provided seeds for the corn, which the Europeans had never seen before. They also helped the English settlers to hunt and fish.

4 Today, Americans celebrate this happy harvest festival on the fourth Thursday of November with much the same food as had been eaten at the first Thanksgiving.

5 The next year no Thanksgiving celebrations were held, and it didn't become an annual event until the 1780s. It was made a national holiday in 1863 by President Abraham Lincoln.

DAY 25 Thanksgiving

1

The Mayflower

In the early 17th century in England, a group of Protestants, known as the Puritans, began to disapprove of the Church of England's sympathies towards the Catholics. The Puritans wanted to change the church from within. But a sub-group, later known as the Separatists, wanted to be totally independent and to found a church of their own. First they went to the Netherlands and then some of these, and others who had remained in England, decided to set up a new church in America. Around 50 Separatists, along with 50 pioneers who wanted a new life and opportunities, then set off from Plymouth, England in 1620 in a ship called the Mayflower. These people later became known as the Pilgrims. They were followed by 14,000 to 20,000 settlers between 1629 and 1642.

The first Thanksgiving

2 Rewriting history?

- Hand out photocopies. The true and false statements are for students to answer after listening.

Listening 2

- Students hear an interview with an American history teacher, who exposes some of the myths behind Thanksgiving.

 **1** T **2** T **3** T **4** T **5** T **6** F

A Good evening and welcome to *One World* for a special Thanksgiving programme. Later in the evening we'll be hearing from Wayne Sharp up in Plymouth Rock. But now I'd like to introduce Lynne Craig, a high school history teacher whose students today have been learning a slightly different version of the traditional Thanksgiving story. Lynne ...

B Thank you, Jeff. I think that what we've been handed down over the generations is the myth of Thanksgiving, what we'd like Thanksgiving to be, rather than the historical facts of it all which have almost become irrelevant or at least very much distorted.

A For political purposes?

B Yes, I think we can draw parallels with pretty much any place where white people have overrun the native inhabitants. We need to distort our history to justify what happened. Politicians needed to appeal to the sense of a melting pot, and of an ideal time when the whites and indigenous people lived happily together.

A But what about those first Pilgrims?

B Well, they've been romanticised out of all proportion. I mean when the Puritans actually gained power in England, that was really the end of music, dance and theatre; for a while at least. They even banned Christmas. And the ones that left for America were really out to build their own Holy Kingdom.

A And the natives they found kind of represented the devil?

B That's it exactly. The Pilgrims were Satan hunters, they were the chosen elect. It wasn't long before they were telling their Indian neighbours that their religion and customs were wrong. And they used anything in their power to achieve their ends – torture, deception, war; some would even say genocide.

A So why were the Wampanoag Indians invited to the Thanksgiving?

B The main reason was to get an agreement out of them which would secure the rights of the Pilgrims to the plantations around Plymouth. And Mather the Elder actually thanked God for sending the plague of smallpox that wiped out many of Wampanoag Indians, who'd actually

been the only reason why the Pilgrims had a harvest to celebrate in the first place, as they'd been the ones that had shown them how to cultivate the land.

A The Wampanoag even brought most of the food, didn't they? Or is that part of the myth too?

B Well, apparently they did. But tonight all around the States people are going to be sitting down to their Thanksgiving meals blissfully unaware of the true meaning of that first Thanksgiving.

3 A generation later ...

- Ask students how modern-day American Indians must feel about their ancestors, about what happened to their ancestors, about what is happening to them in America today. Then ask them to imagine that they are an American Indian who is going to make a short speech to white Americans at Plymouth Rock on Thanksgiving Day – what will they say?

- Students then read the text and answer the questions below. Use this as a basis for discussion on genocide and racism, cross-cultural understanding and utopian society.

2 Rewriting history?

True or false?

1 The Thanksgiving story is more myth than truth.

2 The Europeans and indigenous people never lived happily together.

3 The Puritans were so pure they even banned Christmas in England.

4 The Pilgrims were totally intolerant towards the Wampanoag Indians' religion.

5 The main reason for the Thanksgiving dinner was to get an agreement from the Indians for plantation rights.

6 Unlike in the tradition, the Wampanoag didn't bring most of the food.

A modern Thanksgiving meal

3

A generation later …

A generation later, after the balance of power had indeed shifted, the Indian and white children of that Thanksgiving were striving to kill each other in the genocidal conflict known as King Philip's War. At the end of that conflict most of the New England Indians were either exterminated or became refugees among the French in Canada, or they were sold into slavery in the Carolinas by the Puritans. So successful was this early trade in Indian slaves that several Puritan ship owners in Boston began the practice of raiding the Ivory Coast of Africa for black slaves to sell to the proprietary colonies of the South, thus founding the American-based slave trade.

Today the town of Plymouth Rock has a Thanksgiving ceremony each year in remembrance of the first Thanksgiving. There are still Wampanoag people living in Massachusetts. In 1970, they asked one of them to speak at the ceremony to mark the 350th anniversary of the Pilgrims' arrival. Here is part of what was said:

'Today is a time of celebrating for you – a time of looking back to the first days of white people in America. But it is not a time of celebrating for me. When the Pilgrims arrived, we, the Wampanoags, welcomed them with open arms, little knowing that it was the beginning of the end. That before 50 years were to pass, the Wampanoag would no longer be a tribe. That we and other Indians living near the settlers would be killed by their guns or dead from diseases that we caught from them. Let us always remember, the Indian is and was just as human as the white people. What has happened cannot be changed. But today we work toward a better America, a more Indian America, where people and nature once again are important.'

1 In recent history what other examples of religious intolerance and genocide can you think of? How did these situations arise? How can they be stopped in the future?

2 Imagine that a large number of refugees have come to your neighbourhood. Would you try to make them feel welcome? Would you share your possessions with them? Would you share your home with them?

3 Imagine that you have just settled in a new previously undiscovered land inhabited by only a few indigenous peoples. How would you form your own utopia?

DAY 26 Winter Solstice

Date	December 21 (Northern hemisphere)
	June 21 (Southern hemisphere)
Level	Ex 1 lower intermediate
	Ex 2 upper intermediate
Age	Ex 1 all ages
	Ex 2 adults
Time	Ex 1 10 minutes
	Ex 2 15 minutes
Advice	Not all your students may appreciate learning the pagan origins of Christmas, and some may actually deny them.
Vocabulary	ancestor, slave, master, exclusive, pagan, evergreens, fraternity, moral purity, everlasting life, sacred mushroom

On December 21 the sun is farthest south of the celestial equator, thus giving us our shortest day (see background information to **Day 14: Summer Solstice**).

There is a story that tells how Adam, in his first year of life in the Garden of Eden, had no idea as to why the days started to get shorter. He began to fear that the days were being eaten up by some kind of cosmic snake and that eventually there would only be dark. After the first winter solstice when the process began to reverse he exclaimed, in Greek, *kalon dio* (praise be to God) and hence the new year and the *calendar* began.

This unit is really a pre-Christmas unit, which explains some of the pagan background to the Christmas story. In around 350 AD the date of December 25 was fixed as Christmas and was aimed at suppressing festivals associated with the god Mithras (see the first listening exercise) who the Church associated with the works of Satan. December 25 also coincided with pagan Yuletide celebrations. 'Yule' (a time of revelry, from the same root as 'yawling' or crying out) survives in many languages' words for Christmas (see page 109 in the Appendix).

1 The shortest day

- Hand out photocopies and ask students to answer the questions in groups.
- Alternatively, for question 4, ask students to jot down their own answers on a piece of paper. When they have done this, tell them to go around the class and ask other students what their favourite and least favourite things are. They should add any new things they hear to their own list. See who has the longest list when you stop the activity.

2 Mithras and Yuletide

- Students read the text for interest and in partial preparation for the listening.

Listening

- This is for high levels only. Dictate the following questions.

1 What parallels are there between Mithras and Christ?
2 When was the date of Christmas officially decided?
3 Why was December 25 chosen?
4 What differences with regard to Jesus' birth are there between the gospels of Matthew and Luke?

 1 The virgin birth, resurrection, moral purity, the hope of everlasting life.

2 350 AD.

3 To quash pagan celebrations of the same day.

4 There are differences in the way the news of Jesus' coming birth was announced, and in the question of whether Jesus' parents already lived in Bethlehem or not.

At the same period as the Romans were honouring their god of agriculture at the festival of Saturnalia, the Persians were celebrating their sun-god, Mithras. The parallels between the lives of Mithras and Christ are remarkable. Mithras too was born of a virgin, and, like Christ, was resurrected. The main elements of his faith were fraternity and moral purity, with the hope of everlasting life. The most symbolic and unifying elements were the celebrations of the rebirth of the sun, Sol Invictus, which coincided very nicely with the birth of the Son of God.

The early Christians didn't celebrate Christ's birthday, as birthdays themselves were associated with pagan practices. Although tradition says that people began celebrating Christmas in the year 98, the date of December 25 as the official birthday of Christ was only decided in 350 by the Bishop of Rome, Julius the first. The choice of December 25 was designed to try and quash the pagan celebrations, though it took several centuries to do this.

Nobody actually knows when Christ was born and some scholars deny he even existed. A specialist in oriental studies from Manchester University once claimed that Jesus was the code name for a secret cult of the sacred mushroom. The New Testament is itself full of contradictions. According to Matthew it is Joseph who receives news of Jesus's coming birth in a dream, whereas Luke says that Mary got the news directly from the Angel Gabriel. Luke says that Mary and Joseph had to travel from their home in Nazareth to Bethlehem for the Roman census. But in Matthew's gospel Jesus' parents already lived in Bethlehem and only had to leave to escape King Herod's edict on the killing of children.

If you want to check the gospel stories: Matthew 1.18ff, Luke 2.1ff. One of our famous Christmas carols, *While shepherds watch their flocks by night,* is further evidence of how unlikely December 25 is for the birthday of Jesus, as shepherds simply wouldn't be around with their flocks in that season.

DAY 26 Winter Solstice

1 The shortest day

'On the shortest day it doesn't get light until nine o'clock and by
three o'clock it's nearly dark again.'

(*Britt Kalhagen, Norway*)

1 In your country how many hours of daylight do you have on your shortest day?
2 What kind of problems do you think there must be living in very northern countries?
3 Would you prefer to have a constant number of hours of sun every day all year round?
4 What are the things you like most and least about mid-winter?

2

Mithras and Yuletide

Even on the darkest days of winter we have no doubt that
the sun will soon be getting stronger again and the days longer.
Our ancestors in Europe were not so sure. They had to find
ways of encouraging the sun to restore its energies, by
lighting huge bonfires on the winter solstice.

In the Roman empire people celebrated two main
midwinter festivals. Saturnalia, which began on around
December 17, was named after Saturnus, a god whose name
meant 'plenty' or 'bounty'. Saturnalia was a period of feasting
and present giving, and the world was turned upside down,
with slaves becoming the masters. But there was also a secret
and exclusive Mithraic religion, which was highly influential,
as many of its members were in the army or were Roman
businessmen. They celebrated the Birthday of the
Unconquered Sun (Sol Invictus) on around December 25.

In Anglo-Saxon England, December 25 was the beginning
of the Anglo-Saxon year, and, like most peoples of Northern
Europe, the English celebrated Yuletide. This was a pagan feast
which provided many elements of our modern-day Christmas.
Like the Romans, they decorated their houses with evergreens
as symbols of the continuity of life while other trees and plants
seemed dead. The Scandinavians would bring a huge log (the
Yule log) into the house – it was a symbol of good luck if it
could be kept alight for 12 hours (or 12 days according to some)
And, again like the Romans, they had massive feasts and
drank in vast quantities. The Christians
then converted such habits to their
own use, so that, for example, the
evergreen holly became the symbol
of Christ's crown of thorns.

DAY 27 Christmas

Date	December 25
Level	Ex 1 upper intermediate
	Exs 2–5 intermediate
Age	all ages
Time	Ex 1 5 minutes
	Ex 2 15 minutes
	Ex 3 10 minutes
	Ex 4 15 minutes
	Ex 5 5–10 minutes each game
Grammar	Listening 1 *used to/would* for past habits
Vocabulary	decorate, fairy lights, tinsel, crackers, mistletoe, Christmas pudding, turkey, mantlepiece, stockings, servant, ham, scared, acrobatic stunts, broom, spank, straw, riddle, cookies, sixpence, sack (v), reindeer, sleigh, carol, wrap, Christmas Eve, Boxing Day

1 Christmas origins

- Students read the text for interest.

2 Christmas scene

- Hand out photocopies and focus students' attention on the picture of a typical scene in a house in Britain at Christmas time. Elicit relevant vocabulary (which will be needed for exercise 5) by asking questions like: What's lying under the Christmas tree?

- Then ask the class if in their country this scene might be different and how. Also, ask them to imagine how Christmas might be in Australia or New Zealand, where it falls in the middle of summer.

Listening 1

- Students hear how a New Zealand woman used to celebrate her Christmas. Dictate these questions.

1 How hot was it?
2 What meats did they eat?
3 Where was the Christmas tree?
4 How many guests were there?
5 Where did they eat?
6 What did they do some time after eating?

1 80 °F (about 35 °C)   4 14 to 20.
2 Turkey, lamb and ham.   5 Outside.
3 On the veranda.   6 They went swimming.

We used to go to my grandparents' for Christmas and they lived in a village which didn't have electricity and there was this big wood stove. Now it was 80 degrees during the day, so after midnight service, we'd come home, pop the turkey in and also a couple of legs of lamb, we would have done the ham earlier. Then Christmas Day itself um we had, we used to eat outside. The Christmas tree was always on the veranda. I mean it was all lit up, tinsel and everything, robins everywhere and fairy lights – but it was outside on the veranda. And we would have about oh 14 to 20 people, but we always ate outside and we had a complete mixture. We always had hot turkey, hot lamb, but not hot vegetables no. Then we had huge big bowls of salad, fresh fruit salad. But we also had hot Christmas pudding and brandy butter and custard. I mean it was the most ridiculous menu.

Then, well we couldn't swim straight after that, but generally later on in the afternoon, we'd go down to the lake and have a bit of a swim, you know walk down, walk off the dinner a bit. And of course I once got terribly sunburnt at Christmas, I mean I just just forgot and went to sleep.

3 Christmas quiz

- In groups students try to answer the questions, before listening to the answers on the tape. The answers to question 1 are on page 109 in the Appendix.

Listening 2

- Students hear the answers to the five true and false statements in question 2, but not in the same order. Their task is to match the recorded extracts with the written statements, and also to understand whether the statements were true or false. You might wish to follow it with a few comprehension questions.

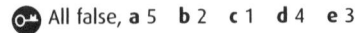 All false, **a** 5 **b** 2 **c** 1 **d** 4 **e** 3

1 On the day after Christmas, collection boxes in churches used to be opened and the money that had been collected was given to the poor. It was also a tradition on this day for working people and servants to break open their tip boxes. These were boxes that contained money that rich people had given them throughout the year.
2 Germans brought the Christmas tree both to Britain, via the royal family, and to the United States, via immigrants. But the habit of decorating trees goes back to the Romans and their festival of Saturnalia.
3 Christmas cards are an English invention and the first one was published in 1843. About a thousand million are sent every year in Britain.
4 Christmas is celebrated in most countries of the world, even where there are only small Christian communities, such as Nigeria, Iran, Iraq, India, Japan and China. But even non-Christians celebrate it as a time of year for giving gifts and generally having a good time.
5 The custom of exchanging gifts at this time of year was already common well before the birth of Christ.

DAY 27 Christmas

1 Christmas origins

Christmas celebrates the birth of Christ, who was probably born between 11 BC and 4 BC (the death of King Herod, who plays a key role in the events surrounding Christ's birth). Some historians try to connect Christ's birth to the famous star that guided the three wise men. If the star were the bright lights of Saturn and Jupiter in conjunction with Pisces, it would make the date 7 BC; however, if it was Halley's Comet, it would have been 11 BC.

Christmas as we know it today is really the work of the Victorians combined with a few traditions imported by the royal family from their native Germany. Until that time Easter had always been the most important festival. In 1652 the Puritans actually banned Christmas.

A number of pagan traditions still survive, such as carol singing, the flames of the Christmas pudding, kissing under the mistletoe, excessive drinking, and bad luck if the Christmas tree is not taken down before the twelfth night.

2 Christmas scene

3 Christmas quiz

1 Can you match these Christmas greetings with their languages?

a	Boas Festas	Esperanto
b	Buon Natale	German
c	Feliz Navidad	Italian
d	Fröhliche Weihnachten	Portuguese
e	Gajan Kristnaskon	Spanish
f	Glaedelig Jul	Danish
g	Hristos se rodi	French
h	Joyeux Noël	Malay
i	Nadolig Llawen	Serbian
j	Selamat Hari Krisna, Dan Tahun Bahru	Welsh

2 **a** Exchanging Christmas presents derives from the three kings/wise men's example. (T/F)

b The Christmas tree is a fairly recent invention. (T/F)

c In Britain December the 26th is known as Boxing Day, as there is an annual boxing competition on this day. (T/F)

d Christmas is only celebrated by Christians. (T/F)

e Christmas cards are a derivation of a pre-Christian Jewish custom. (T/F)

4 Santa Claus

The original Santa Claus, or Saint Nicholas, was the Bishop of Smyrna (in what is now Turkey). He lived in the 4th century AD. He is remembered on 6 December for his generosity and love to children – he used to throw children gifts through their windows. His fame spread to Russia, Scandinavia and many parts of Europe.

Meanwhile in England, following the spirit of Saturnalia (a festival left behind by the Romans), masters served their servants at Christmas time, and people generally had a good time drinking and playing jokes on each other. The figure of Father Christmas grew out of these festivities. He was someone who, like Santa Claus, tried to help the poor and children.

Victorian children were the first to send messages to Father Christmas, saying not just what they wanted for Christmas, but also confessing their sins and renewing old promises.

The story of Santa Claus was brought to America by Dutch immigrants and was a variation of the Dutch Sinter Klaas. Nowadays in Britain the names Father Christmas and Santa Claus are used interchangeably.

- Hand out photocopies and ask students to read the text and the letters to Santa Claus. Then tell them to imagine that Santa Claus really exists and that he could give them anything they wanted (not necessarily just presents, but also abstract things such as more intelligence, artistic talent). They should write him a letter with a list of four things they would really like.

- Then ask them to compare their list with other students and explain their choices.

Listening 3

- Students hear a Dutch girl (authentic recording, she spent a long time in Canada) recounting the origins of the Dutch Sinter Klaas (though how he ended up coming on a boat from Spain is anybody's guess!). Students listen and answer the same questions as on the photocopies. Tell them that not all the questions are answered. Lower levels can simply mark the questions that are answered.

 1 Yes.

  2 Spain.

  3 He has a white horse and black helpers.

  4 He is dressed in red.

  5 You write poems and sing songs. You have to leave a carrot and straw for the horse and cookies for Sinter Klaas.

  6 Not mentioned.

  7 Yes.

  8 He spanks you, takes you back to Spain in a bag and you have to pick oranges for him. And you don't get a present.

  9 Not mentioned.

It's called Sinter Klaas and it's celebrated on December the fifth. And it's a nice tall man all in a red dress. And he comes on a big boat with his black helpers and they do all acrobatic stunts and stuff. And they walk around with these big *juten* bags. And the thing is the children are all really scared of Sinter Klaas because if you're bad he will take you back to Spain. [To Spain?] Yes, that's where he comes from. And then for the rest of the year you have to pick oranges for him. If you're good you get sweets and if you're bad he'll take you back in a bag or he gives you – he'll spank your bum with the end of a broom, we call it the *roe*.

So and it's ... you have to write poems and sing songs in front of the fireplace and you have to put a wooden shoe with a carrot and straw because he comes also on his white horse and he rides over the top of the roofs. So in the evening you have to sing really loud and ask him to come by your house and tell him that you've been a good girl or a good boy. And so you leave that for him and you also leave cookies for him and his helpers. And then in the morning the carrot is gone and the cookies are gone and you find a gift if you've been a good girl or a good boy.

Follow-up

- Students tell each other what they are going to buy for their family and friends for Christmas.

- Alternatively, from glossy magazines cut out some advertisements for gifts, and put each gift on an individual card. Divide the class into groups and give each group an assortment of cards. Students decide which gifts they would like to give and receive and why. In multinational classes students can discuss gifts which are typically given in their country.

5 Christmas games

- On pages 88–89 there are a few games to get students in a Christmas mood. Linguistic content was not my prime motivation in compiling these games.

1 Spot the difference

- The two pictures on pages 85 and 88 have ten differences. Put students in pairs and make sure they have different pictures. Instruct them to find the ten differences by asking each other questions.

 The key to the Christmas games is in the Appendix.

Christmas carols

- On pages 109 and 110 are the words of a few English carols and songs. Students can sing along with these old favourites. If you want to set them a task, you could blank out the odd word here and there for them to write in as they listen.

4 Santa Claus

Father Christmas.

On Christmas Eve, the night before Christmas, Father Christmas goes round every childs house and brings them toys. You have to write him a letter to say what toys you want. You put the letter on your fireplace so it will blow up your chimney. He might bring you those things you want if you are good. Father Christmas has some messengers. They are fairies. Before Christmas you have to be good because you can not see the tiny fairies, and on Christmas Eve the fairies tell Father Christmas if you are good. Father Christmas has different names like Santa Claus and Saint Nicholas.

Dear Santa
I hope you are well. I have had a fun year and tried hard to be good. Please will you bring me

a new bicycle
a pair of rollerblades
a puppy
a CD player
and some sweets

Happy Christmas

Love, Sophie

Dear Father Christmas
I hope you think I've been good because I have. When you come I will put out a mince pie for you and carrots for the reindeers. Please bring me a train set, soldiers, pens and a ball.
from
Kynan

1 Is there a fictitious person in your country who gives presents?
2 Where does he/she come from?
3 Does he/she have any animals or helpers?
4 How is he/she dressed?
5 What preparations have to be made for this event – food, stockings, etc?
6 What role do the parents take?
7 Are the children scared of him/her?
8 What happens if you are a bad child?
9 Do you remember when and how you discovered that this person didn't really exist?

5 Christmas games

1 Spot the difference

2 Christmas wordsearch

*Can you find the 16 Christmas words hidden in the wordsearch? You can go across,
down or diagonally left to right. The same letter cannot belong to more than two words.*

C	C	H	W	H	I	T	E	F	R
S	A	M	C	R	M	E	S	E	E
A	R	I	P	R	A	S	T	S	I
N	D	S	G	U	A	P	O	T	N
T	C	T	S	I	D	C	C	I	D
A	A	L	U	L	F	D	K	V	E
Y	R	E	A	R	E	T	I	E	E
I	O	T	R	U	K	I	N	N	R
R	L	O	S	T	S	E	G	M	G
E	V	E	P	A	R	T	Y	H	A

CARD
CAROL
CRACKER
EVE
FESTIVE
GIFT
MISTLETOE
PARTY
PUDDING
REINDEER
SANTA CLAUS
SLEIGH
STOCKING
TURKEY
WHITE
WRAP

3 Christmas crackers

British people have fun pulling crackers over Christmas lunch or dinner. The crackers explode when you pull them and inside you find a silly party hat, a useless gadget (such as keyrings, plastic earrings) and a joke or a riddle. Here are four riddles for you to solve:

1 Which is the one and only word spelt incorrectly in this sentence?

2 The more you take away from it, the larger it becomes; the more you add to it, the smaller it becomes. What is it?

3 What is it that was given to you, belongs to you excusively, and yet is used more by your friends than by yourself?

4 What is it that no one wishes to have, yet no one wishes to lose?

4

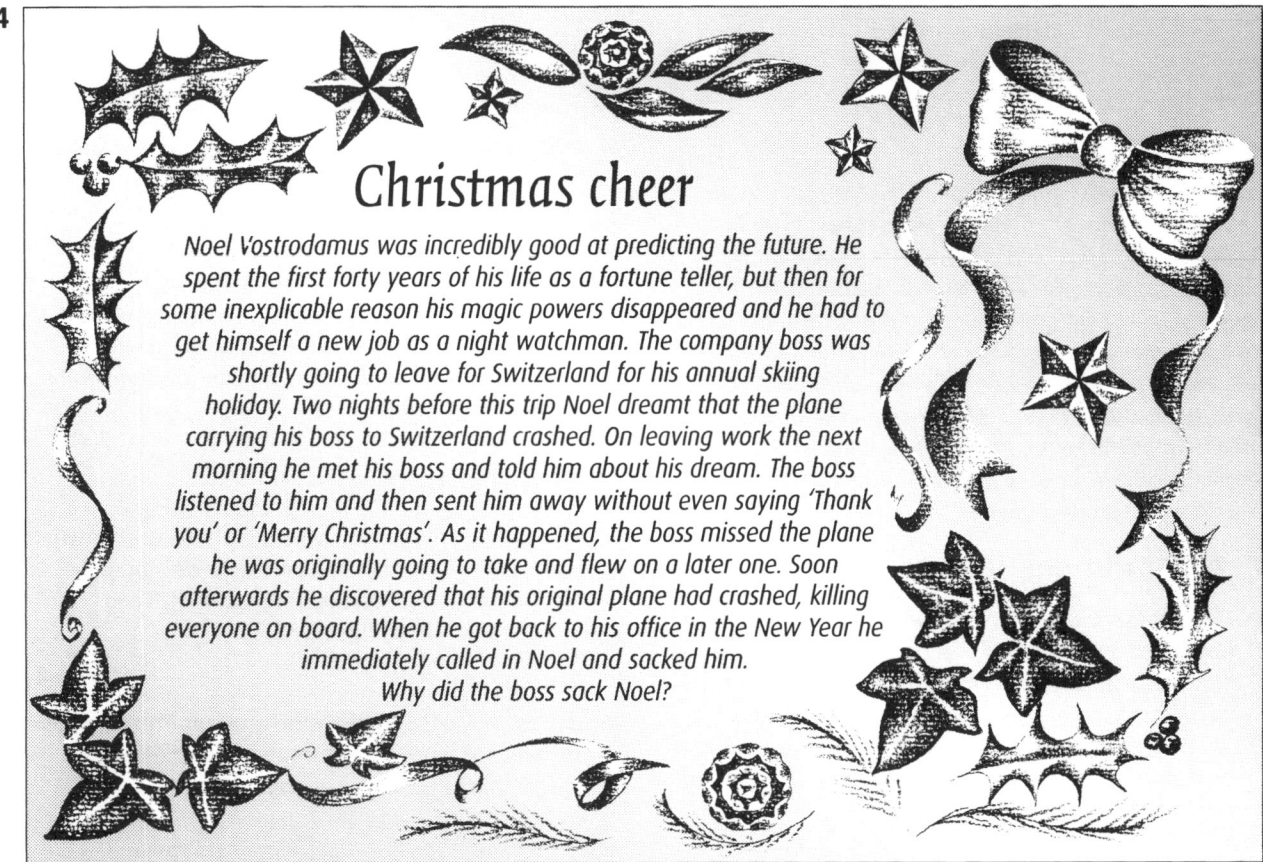

Christmas cheer

Noel Vostrodamus was incredibly good at predicting the future. He spent the first forty years of his life as a fortune teller, but then for some inexplicable reason his magic powers disappeared and he had to get himself a new job as a night watchman. The company boss was shortly going to leave for Switzerland for his annual skiing holiday. Two nights before this trip Noel dreamt that the plane carrying his boss to Switzerland crashed. On leaving work the next morning he met his boss and told him about his dream. The boss listened to him and then sent him away without even saying 'Thank you' or 'Merry Christmas'. As it happened, the boss missed the plane he was originally going to take and flew on a later one. Soon afterwards he discovered that his original plane had crashed, killing everyone on board. When he got back to his office in the New Year he immediately called in Noel and sacked him.
Why did the boss sack Noel?

5 Christmas pudding

Before the metric system was introduced, parents used to put silver sixpences into the Christmas pudding, which lucky members of the family would find (if they didn't swallow them!). Place ten coins as shown. Then turn the pyramid upside down by moving three coins, one at a time.

DAY 28 Birthdays

Date	varies
Level	Exs 2, 3 intermediate
	Exs 1, 4, 5 upper intermediate
Age	all ages, especially teenagers
Time	Ex 1 15 minutes
	Ex 2 15 minutes
	Ex 3 20 minutes
	Ex 4 10 minutes
	Ex 5 15 minutes
Grammar	Ex 3 modals of permission
Advice	Use this unit either on your own birthday, or on one of your students' birthdays. Make sure you know your students' birthdays at the beginning of the year, then you could surprise them.
Vocabulary	horoscope, aspiration, extroverted, affable, introverted, wary, frank, hemmed in, voting age, low income, afford, Muslim, spot (v), pepper, mature, adolescent, cope with, infant mortality, discount, survival, tribe, expectations, circumstances, epithet

In her book *Birthdays*, which I read while researching the subject, Linda Rannells Lewis had this to say: 'When I began to see how birthdays served a wide range of personal and social functions, I wondered if a longer look at this taken-for-granted ritual might provide unusual insights into how we celebrate ourselves, remember ourselves as children, gauge our effect on others, reckon our worth, allow ourselves pleasure or twist ourselves into painful knots, how we come to know ourselves or avoid self knowledge.' With older students you might initiate a discussion on how we feel about our birthdays as we get older and whether at a later stage in life birthdays serve any purpose.

1 Your birth and the zodiac

- If you think your students are into astrology, then **the lesson before** doing this unit on Birthdays, ask all students what their date of birth is (noting this down on a piece of paper, so that you seem really serious) and tell them you are an expert in astrology and that next lesson you are going to give them a personalised horoscope.

- Next lesson, give each student a copy of the Personality Profile on page 111 preferably with the student's individual name on. Tell them not to show their piece of paper to anyone (otherwise they might realise they're reading the same piece). Pre-teach any vocabulary, then tell them not to ask any questions while they're reading (again to avoid suspicion).

- Ask students how well the paragraph describes them.

- Now hand out photocopies and ask students to listen and complete the table.

When people read the piece and believe that it has been written specially for them, they all say the same thing: 'It's me! It describes me exactly!' Why should this be so? Two psychologists, Snider and Shenkel, point out that this description is vague enough to apply to almost everyone, positive enough to please almost everyone, and flattering enough to get almost anyone to accept it. As research shows, the more effort people invest in getting a horoscope or profile, the more likely they are to believe the results – even when the identical results are given to everyone. If they must pay money for a profile, take the time to write away for it, or give detailed and specific information about themselves, they are more likely to believe the profile is 'eerily accurate'. A French psychologist once advertised himself as an astrologer. In reply to the hundreds of people who wrote to him for his services, he sent out the same vague horoscope. More than two hundred grateful clients took the time to write thank-you notes praising his accuracy and perceptiveness.

Listening 1

- Students hear five people saying when they were born, what star sign they are, and whether they are typical of it.

📼 The tapescript is given on page 111 in the Appendix.

- Finally, students discuss the four questions in groups.

Follow-up

- In multicultural classes get students to discuss the traditions associated with birth in their culture, e.g. what brings good and bad luck, what religious rites are involved and how soon they take place, what celebrations there are, if there are any differences between girls and boys.

2 Birthday parties

- Ask students to tell each other about the best or worst birthday they have ever had, about parties they have been to, and presents they have received. Then proceed to the listening exercise.

Listening 2

- Students fill in the table while listening. You can then use this as a basis for discussion on birthdays and ages for voting in their country.

1 F   **2** T   **3** 15 (girls)   **4** 21 (though 18 is becoming increasingly popular)   **5** 18   **6** 16, 18   **7** 18, 21   **8** unmarried 30-year-olds   **9** 88

📼 The tapescript is given on page 112 in the Appendix.

DAY 28 Birthdays

1 Your birth and the zodiac

	date of birth	star sign	characteristics
Speaker 1			
Speaker 2			
Speaker 3			
Speaker 4			
Speaker 5			

1 What are the typical characteristics of people of your sign?
Do you share those characteristics?

2 Do you believe that your life is influenced in any way by your star sign?

3 Have you noticed that your friends or lovers share the same star sign?

4 Do you regularly read your horoscope? If not, why not?

2 Birthday parties

True or false?

1 All cultures celebrate birthdays.

2 The early Christian church was against celebrating birthdays.

Most important birthday in ...

3 Argentina and Mexico:

4 Britain:

5 Finland:

Voting age in ...

6 Senegal (female):   (male):

7 Bangladesh (female):   (male):

Special 30th birthday party in Norway

8 For who:

Luckiest birthday in Japan

9 Age:

3 Stages of life

- Ask students to fill in columns **A** and **B** in the table and then to discuss their answers.

Listening 3

- Students hear four children/young adults (American, Irish, English, Anglo-Italian) describing the good and bad things about being a particular age. Students should put a cross in the appropriate column (1–4) against the items that the speakers mention they can't do and a tick against the ones they can do. Then ask students which speakers mention their ages, and how old they are.

	1	2	3	4
... decide when to go to bed				✗
... do paid work				
... drink alcohol		✗	✔	
... drive	✗	✗	✔	
... smoke			✔	
... go wherever you want	✗			
... watch whatever you want on TV				
... get reduced prices at the cinema		✗		
... get reduced prices on public transport		✗		

Their ages are: **1** (not mentioned, in reality she's 12)
2 16   **3** 20   **4** 7

1 Your parents get to tell you what to do and you don't have as much and you're not allowed to do as much things as your parents are. Like you can't drive cars, and you can't always go places that you want to go.

2 I don't think there's anything good about being sixteen. Because, when you're fifteen, you're ... you get ... it's cheaper on the buses and into the cinemas and everything. And um all the things you can't do at 15 you still can't do at 16. But when you're 16 the price for the bus doubles and for the train, and into cinemas, you don't get a discount anymore. So ... and you can't drive a car until you're 17, and you can't drink until you're 18, so there's nothing really very good about being 16.

3 The things that I like about being 20. Well, I suppose I can drink, and I can smoke and I can drive, not all at once of course. And I think it's a good age, but if I was in America, you can't drink or do a lot of things until you're 21, but, so I'm glad that I live in England.

4 I'm seven years old. The bad things are that I can't stay up late, I can't watch television up late. My daddy makes me read. And the good things are that I can play and I don't have to work, I mean jobs.

- Focus attention on the last speaker, who specifically mentions some bad and good things about being this age. Then refer students to the first question and give them a few minutes to discuss it. On the board make a table of pros and cons of a particular age (perhaps the average age of the students in the class) and fill it in with the help of your students.

- Finally, students can discuss the other questions.

4 Names

- This exercise can be done either on someone's birthday or alternatively on their 'name day' if they have one, e.g. saints' days in Catholic countries.

- Students simply read the text and answer the questions.

3 Stages of life

How old are you when (A) you are allowed to, and (B) you think you should be allowed to ...

	A	B	1	2	3	4
... decide when to go to bed?						
... do paid work?						
... drink alcohol?						
... drive?						
... go wherever you want?						
... smoke?						
... watch whatever you want on TV?						

Up to what age (A) can you, and (B) should you ...

	A	B	1	2	3	4
... get reduced prices at the cinema?						
... get reduced prices on public transport?						

1 What are the good and bad things about being your particular age?
2 At what age do we conform most closely to people of the same age and reject our parents' values?
3 When do we have to cope with the biggest changes in our life?
4 Who feels the most isolated – adolescents or old people?
5 How many stages of life do you think there are? Which is the best stage? And the worst?

4

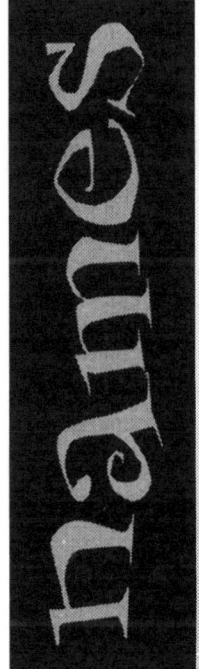

Various cultures name their children in different ways. In many Catholic countries children are often named after saints, in fact some priests will not allow parents to name their children after soap opera stars or football players. Protestant countries tend to be more free about this, however in Norway certain names, such as Adolf, are banned completely.

In countries where infant mortality is very high, such as in Africa, tribes only name their children when they reach five years old, the age in which their chances of survival begin to increase. Until that time they are referred to by the number of years they are. These tribes and many nations in the Far East give their children a unique name (i.e. no one else has the same name) which in some way describes the circumstances of the child's birth or the parents' expectations and hopes for the child.

Some Australian aborigines can keep changing their name throughout their life as the result of some important experience which has in some way proved their wiseness, creativity or determination. For example, if one day one of them dances extremely well, he or she may decide to re-name him/herself 'supreme dancer' or 'light feet'.

1 How were you given your name? Do you like it?
2 Do you have a 'name day' in your culture?
3 Does your name have an equivalent in English? If you could have an English name what name would you choose?
4 If you could name yourself like the aborigines, i.e. with some kind of description, what epithet would you choose?

5 Rites of passage

- Students read the text and then answer the questions.

Most Catholics have their first major rite (apart from baptism) at the age of seven. At the time of writing the Anglican church is thinking of letting seven-year-olds take communion, rather than the current age of 14. By doing so the Church also hopes to reduce falling attendances.

Listening 4

- Play the piece once and ask students to guess what the boy is doing and what religion he is.

○━ He is an English Jewish boy reciting the Sedra for his Bar Mitzvah.

Listening 5

- Students hear a Jewish boy describing the Bar Mitzvah ceremony. Pre-teach: Rabbi, deed, sin. Students listen once and match the questions on their page with the listening extracts.

○━ **1** a **2** c **3** d **4** e **5** f **6** b

- Then they listen again and try to answer the questions.

○━ **a** 13, reading the Sedra
  b Yes.
  c The Torah.
  d Yes, boys 13; girls 12.
  e To mark when you turn into a man (woman).
  f You become responsible for your own deeds.

1 It's tradition that when you're thirteen years old you reach the Bar Mitzvah age which traditionally means that you reach the age of being a man, and you have to go to Shul on that day and you have to recite the Sedra which you've already prepared. You read the Sedra, it's specially ... , you're told about a year before which Sedra you have, so you're given time to prepare it, you prepare it with your Rabbi, and in my case, I prepared it with my father, because that was what he liked to do.

2 The Sedra is the reading of the Torah, and it's split up into the five books of the Torah.

3 It's mainly for the boys, but over the last century they've introduced something called a Bat Chayil which is for the girls, and they say that when they reach the age of 12, because they're supposed to be more mature than boys, then the same thing happens.

4 It's, it's, they say it's because you turn into a man, this is what happens, and every Jewish boy does it.

5 We're told that after you've done it, every good deed that you did before the age of thirteen goes to your father, and if you do something bad then it goes on your father your father's record, so that when he dies and goes to heaven then that's on his record. But now that you're thirteen, you hold your own sins so that and they say a special blessing after the call up and the father frees you of him, basically saying that, you know, now you have to hold your own sins, do your own deeds.

6 Usually you have a party afterwards on the Sunday night or the Saturday night, and something beforehand for the family and friends. You get presents then.

5

Rites of passage

Different cultures identify different attributes as those appropriate for adulthood. In Central America there are tribes in which warfare and honour are the prime necessities for manhood, and self-torture is required to prove one's capacity for the role of honourable warrior. In Australia there are tribes where adulthood means the separation of the sexes and the creation of a dominant, self-sufficient, male cult.

A first communion

A Bar Mitzvah ceremony

There are a number of ways to mark the change from childhood. The Nandi boys and girls of East Africa have their heads shaved and are given an emetic to remove all traces of their former life. Others cast off their old clothes. A few are beaten, tortured, starved, frightened. At the end of this trial it is no wonder that a young person may feel so shaken up and broken apart and put back together again that he feels like a different person. He is ritually reborn. He sees the world as if for the first time, with new understanding, new responsibility, new status, new clothes, a new name, a new value to his family.

Dinka initiation ceremony, South Sudan

a At what age do you have particular rites in your culture? What do these rites consist of?
b Do you have some kind of party or receive presents?
c What is the name of your religious book?
d Are there different rites for boys and girls? Do they take place at different ages?
e Why do you have these rites?
f What responsibilities do you have after the ceremony that you don't have before?

DAY 29 Wedding Day

Date	varies
Level	Exs 1, 3, 4, 5 upper intermediate
	Ex 2 intermediate
Ages	Exs 1, 2, 5 all ages
	Exs 3, 4 adults
Time	Ex 1 25 minutes
	Ex 2 10 minutes
	Ex 3 10 minutes
	Ex 4 20 minutes
	Ex 5 15 minutes
Vocabulary	tomb, slave, dormitory, dowry, inheritance, engagement, divorce, alliance, registry office, stag night, hen party, arranged marriage, proposal, chaperone, wedlock, abundance, trial period, capture, misconception, (prison) sentence, ritual, career pressure, fertility, statistic, vein, physical/verbal abuse, prevalent, step-parent, no win situation, infidelity, gambling

1 Ancient and modern

- Brainstorm with students to find out all the words they associate with weddings – the rites and people involved. Students then read the text and answer the questions.

Egyptian men may not have married their sisters, since the word 'sister' may have been the equivalent of our modern day mistress or lover. Christianity took over virtually all aspects of the Roman wedding ceremony.

Listening 1

- Students will hear about marriage in India and Bangladesh. After listening once, they tick the questions on their page that are answered in the listening passage. Then they listen again and write the answers to the questions they ticked.

4 300–400 guests

5 20–50% of the bride's family's savings

6 The parents, but the couple do have a choice.

7 Couples learn to love each other; they have a strong economic base.

8 Yes.

A With the royal wedding tomorrow, *One World* dedicates tonight's programme to a discussion of wedding ceremonies around the world. I'd like to welcome back Shaheen Haq. [Thank you Sarah.] But let's begin with our other guest, Nate Hancock. [Hi.] Nate, you've just got a book out on weddings called *Holy Wedlock*.

C Yes, actually the 'lock' in 'wedlock' has nothing to do with the prison effect of marriage at all. 'Lock' should really be 'lac' which means 'present' or 'gift', which is obviously connected to the dowry system of our ancestors.

A Shaheen, do dowries still exist in India?

B Yes, they do. In fact many Indian families spend between twenty and fifty per cent of their savings on the wedding ceremony, which includes the dowry that the woman's family gives to the man.

C That sounds an incredible lot.

B Well, they invite about three or four hundred relatives and friends to the wedding.

A And are marriages still arranged? [B Yes, they are]

C I was ... Sorry, I just wanted to say that I was talking with a man from Bangladesh who told me that marriages there are arranged but that you can have a kind of trial period after you get married, between one and six months, and then get divorced if you're not compatible.

A That's interesting. And Bangladesh is a Muslim country, right?

C Yes, I think we tend to assume that Muslim countries don't allow divorce, which is just not true. But in any case the man told me that only about five per cent of the marriages don't work out, which if you compare that to the States, where about fifty per cent of marriages end in divorce, that's pretty good.

A Shaheen, was your marriage arranged?

B No, I'm married to an English guy, so, no, it wasn't. But I think there are a lot of misconceptions about arranged marriages. The process is actually the reverse of a typical western marriage which begins with the couple madly in love and then often ends in tears, whereas in India and other countries the couple obviously don't know each other at all at the beginning and then gradually learn to love each other, genuinely too.

C And of course they have the benefit of a strong economic base which is one thing less to worry about.

A And how are the marriages actually arranged?

B Well, back in India the man's parents generally look around for a suitable girl. Then they find out about her family. Then sometimes the couple meet, but always with a chaperone, and they ask each other a few questions. Then the actual wedding takes place at the girl's house and lasts up to three or four days.

A But do the couple have any choice in the matter?

B Of course they do, because it's to everyone's benefit that the marriage works out. But then there are some cases where marriages are forced on people.

Ancient and modern

In ancient Egypt some men, especially the kings, were permitted to have more than one wife. Tomb paintings show that harems existed and that brothers sometimes married sisters.

In ancient Greece, marriages between slaves were recognised by the law. But the children of such marriages belonged to the owners of the children's parents. In theory, free citizens were not allowed to marry slaves.

At a Spartan wedding the bride's hair was cut short and she wore male clothes. After the first night, the husband could only visit his wife secretly and then return to his all-male dormitory. The couple were only allowed to have a house together after several years of marriage.

For the Romans, and most ancient societies, marriage's two main aims were to have children and to control and protect ownership of wealth through alliances, dowries and inheritance. Marriages were arranged by the parents, to the benefit of both families. The decision was usually celebrated by an engagement party, at which agreements (marriage contracts) and gifts were exchanged. Divorce was allowed, and laws stipulated who got what afterwards (the dowry was often returned to the bride's family).

In modern Britain, people from a Christian background either get married in church or in a Registry Office. When they decide to get married they have a period of engagement, and the man generally buys the woman a ring. On the night before the wedding, the man often has a party with his male friends (known as a Stag Night) and the woman has a Hen Party with her female friends. On the day of the wedding it is supposed to bring bad luck if the bridegroom sees his bride before she comes into the church. The bride herself is traditionally dressed in white, though she also wears for good luck something borrowed, something blue, something old and something new.

1 What is the main purpose of marriage in your country?
2 Who makes the proposal for marriage, and how?
3 Do you have engagement parties? When do you exchange presents?
4 How are wedding invitations given? How many guests are usually invited?
5 How much is spent on wedding ceremonies? Who pays?
6 Do you or your parents decide on who you can marry?
7 Are there any advantages of arranged marriages?
8 Are dowries common?
9 What rituals are associated with the night before and the night after the wedding?
10 How do people dress and wear their hair for weddings?

2 Wedding customs

- Hand out photocopies and ask students to look at the illustrations. Elicit wedding dress, honeymoon, marriage, etc.

Listening 2

- Students now hear the origins of four of the five customs illustrated. They should match what they hear with the illustrations.

- You can ask comprehension questions later if you wish.

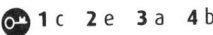 **1** c **2** e **3** a **4** b

1 People used to throw grain or rice at the newly wed couple. This was symbolic of good luck, fertility and abundance.

2 In primitive times a future husband often chose a bride from another tribe. He and his men would then go into enemy territory and capture her. He then left his men there to fight the angry relatives. It generally took the enemy a month, the cycle of a moon, to give up looking for the bride. During this time the husband and his new wife fled and hid in a cave where they would drink a very nutrient honey mixture.

3 The Romans believed that the vein in the third finger led directly to the heart. Medieval Italians used to buy their brides diamond rings, since in folklore diamonds were said to be created from the flames of love. As the singer Madonna once said: Italians do it better.

4 Food has always been an integral part of wedding ceremonies and there is probably no such thing as the first wedding cake. The Romans used to break a cake made of grain on the bride's head; the seeds represented fertility and abundance.

3 Words of wisdom?

- Students fill in the spaces in the quotations with the appropriate words. Make sure they understand the difference between a wedding (i.e. the ceremony) and marriage (the state).

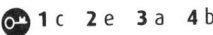 **1** woman, marry, man (Benjamin Disraeli)

   2 wife (Thomas Fuller)

   3 woman, man (feminist graffiti)

   4 married, marriages (Nietzsche)

   5 wife (quoted in Vivien Foster)

   6 weddings, wedding (Brendan Behan)

   7 married (W. Somerset Maugham)

   8 marriage (from King Vidor's silent film *The Crowd* 1928)

Without exception the quotations are cynical in their portrayal of marriage. This was not deliberate – in my five books of quotations I couldn't find one quotation (from over 200) which had a good word to say about marriage.

The word 'marry' derives from the Latin *maritus* (husband), whence Italian *marito* and French *mari*; whereas the Italian word for marriage, *matrimonio*, comes from the Latin *mater* meaning 'mother' – is this a significant difference I ask myself! 'Bride' comes from a Greek verb meaning 'to teem' (in the old sense of 'to produce offspring') and is allied to the Irish *bru*, a womb. The word 'groom' comes from the Anglo-Saxon *guma* (itself a cognate of *homo*), so 'bridegroom' simply meant the 'bride's man'. Husband literally means 'housebound' and tells us that in Anglo-Saxon times it was his obligations to his house (and later by extension to his land – the obsolete word 'husbandman' meant 'tiller of the soil') rather than to his wife that defined a husband's role. 'Wife' originally meant 'woman' (in fact in modern German and other languages the words for husband and wife are the same as for man and woman), which survives in 'midwife' and 'housewife'. The Italian word for wife, *moglie*, comes from the Latin *mungo*, 'I milk', as it was their job to milk the cows. In fact, the Sanskrit root word *duh* (which also means 'to milk') gave us both *moglie* and the English, German, Greek and Slavic words for 'daughter'.

2 Wedding customs

3 Words of wisdom?

Where appropriate insert the words *married* and *marry*, and *marriage*, *wedding*, *man*, *woman*, *husband* and *wife* (either singular or plural forms).

1 Every _____ should _____ – and no _____ .

2 Choose a _____ rather by your ear than your eye.

3 A _____ needs a _____ like a fish needs a bicycle.

4 If _____ couples did not live together, happy _____ would be far more frequent.

5 If you wish to ruin yourself, marry a rich _____ .

6 I think _____ are sadder than funerals, because they remind you of your own _____ . You can't be reminded of your own funeral because it hasn't happened.

7 If people waited to know each other before they _____ , the world wouldn't be so overpopulated as it is now.

8 Take it from me, _____ isn't a word – it's a sentence.

4 Some statistics

- Hand out photocopies and ask students to look at the divorce statistics (rounded figures from around 1996). As a whole class they should think why divorces are more common in some countries than in others.

- Then ask them to put the causes of divorce in order of frequency/commonness.

🔑 They are in fact already in order.

Listening 3

- Students hear some reasons for divorce. They should note down any reasons that are on the list on their page, plus any others.

🔑 career pressures, drinking, violence, arguments, [married too young]

A Well, it seems like divorce is a growing phenomenon all over certainly the western world. I mean, Laurel, it seems to be the most prevalent in the United States, or is that right? It seems to be quite high.

B Do you thing that's true? I don't know that it's more prevalent than anywhere else really. I've heard it's about 50%, I think, of marriages end in divorce, and I wouldn't be surprised if in Europe that's not similar. But I think in the States um there's such career pressures that I think people end up hardly ever seeing each other, which is certainly going to lead to ... , especially if you have two people working – the man and the woman in the relationship working. That's going to be incredibly hard if you never have time to talk to each other, to spend time with each other. And there's always that pressure to move the next step up on the career ladder. I would say, certainly in urban areas, that's a big factor for divorce.

A What, what about you? Do you think, I mean there's, what about the factors for divorce over here? I mean ... would you say there are ... , would you say it's ... , do you know many people who've been divorced? Have you got many friends whose ...

C I've got several friends, that their parents have been divorced, and um it was mainly, the common the common reasons that always came out were um drinking problems with the father [right] was often really high um which is quite a main thing in this country anyway is alcohol [right]. I notice when going over to the States, there's not as much alcohol around [that's true] it's always been a problem here.

A Well, at least it's not, you can't go around on the streets so much drinking [exactly] but certainly in the house, in the home you can certainly drink as much as anywhere else in the world I think.

C And also leads to other things like physical violence often gets. And, you know and people, and leads to the um continual arguments always

happens and the parents get upset with each other and then they take it out on the children, the children get wound up in it [yeah] it's just a no win situation. [yeah]

D I think one thing leads to another, doesn't it? I know someone whose parents, the mother was working during the day and in the evening. And the father was working – just during the day. And when he came home there was no one there, so there was no communication at all, so the dad would go out drinking and the mum would come home and he'd be drunk, and it was probably going to end in divorce I would have thought.

A I mean is it a bad, I mean we look at divorce as being an embarrassing statistic, you know, the high divorce rate, but is it a bad thing if unhappy marriages are made to end? I mean ...

D I think sometimes it's not the fault of the people involved. I mean this couple had been together since they were 16 and they stayed together for 25 years, but they lost all their childhood and they wanted to recapture that when they were older.

A Well that sounds fair enough.

B That's interesting, so there's something to be said about the fact that we do we do have choice now, we can actually, you know people do get married older. I mean I do think that's probably a better idea, really.

D If you get married too young.

B Yeah, that just. You know you need to grow, you need to change with each other, and that's very hard to do.

From my (somewhat limited) investigations, the number of marriages and divorces seems to fluctuate quite considerably from decade to decade in certain countries. For example, in 1920, 1950 and 1960 nearly the same number of people got married in the UK, but there were 30% more divorces in 1950 than in 1960. In Japan today 6.4 people per 1000 get married each year, as against 8.1 in 1925 and 9.5 in 1961.

5 For better or for worse?

- Students read the extract from the marriage service and then, in groups, work out their list of ten ingredients for a successful marriage. They can use some of the ideas in the box if they wish.

- Finally, ask students to invent their own wedding vows.

4 Some statistics

The table below shows the number of marriages (M) and divorces (D) per 1000 inhabitants. The statistics can be interpreted as follows: for every eight marriages in China, one will end in divorce.

	M	D
Brazil	5	0.5
China	8	1
France	4.5	2
Germany	5.5	2
Israel	6.5	1.5
Japan	6.5	1.5
Mexico	8	0.5
Russia	7.5	4.5
Singapore	8.5	1.5
South Korea	7	1
Spain	5	0.5
Sweden	4	2.5
UK	6	3
USA	8	5

Causes of marital discord and breakdown
lack of communication
continual arguments
infidelity
sexual problems
physical and verbal abuse/violence
financial problems
work/career (one partner devoting excessive time)
children (whether to have them, upbringing)
addiction (to drinking, gambling, spending, etc.)
step-parenting

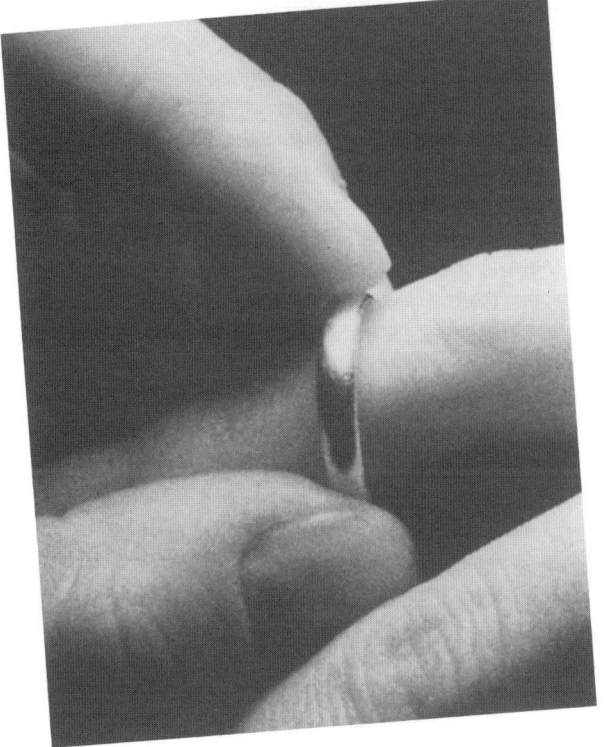

5 For better or for worse?

I take thee to my wedded husband/wife, to have and to hold from this day forward, for better or for worse, for richer for poorer, in sickness and in health, to love and to cherish, till death us do part.

similar age	fidelity
both partners working	similar views on children
common interests	lack of money problems
same race/class/background	no interfering in-laws
fair division of housework	ability to express feelings

DAY 30 Days of the Week

Date	any
Level	Exs 1–3 upper intermediate
	Ex 4 intermediate
Age	all ages
Time	Ex 1 10 minutes
	Ex 2 15 minutes
	Ex 3 20 minutes
Vocabulary	market, god, planet, thunder, civilisation, concept, cycle, derive, mythology, resolve, assembly, fast (v)

The Oxford English Dictionary and Webster's (USA) both still define Sunday as being the first day of the week. Italian dictionaries of over 100 years ago put Monday as the first day, though specifying that for the Church Sunday was still the first. For many Muslims Saturday is the first day.

Defining what a day is is not easy – does it mean hours of light as opposed to night? Is it a specific period of time known to the speakers (e.g. We had a lovely day out. Have you had a good day, darling?)? Or is it 24 hours? The reason it's so difficult to define is that the concept of a day as being 24 hours is only quite recent, and most languages, rather than adopting a totally new word to describe this period, carried on using the rather vague word 'day' which for most of them began when the sun rose and so varied in length at different times of the year. Days used to be counted in terms of 'suns', 'sleeps' and 'dawns', or indeed 'nights' hence the Teutonic 'fortnight' (fourteen nights). A nation's method of telling the time is often reflected in that nation's language, so the Irish word for 'morning' originally meant 'the time when the oxen are unyoked'. In Northern Scandinavia, time was calculated by the position of the sun over the mountain peaks. In English we divide up the day in terms of natural events: daybreak, sunrise, morning.

Before they came into contact with the Romans, the Germanic tribes probably didn't divide up their months into weeks, so what they called a 'week' had a wider meaning than simply a space of seven days. The Indo-European root *weig* literally meant 'bend' with a basic sense of 'a period of change'. In the primitive calendar, months began on the first day of the new moon, in fact it's not difficult to see that 'month' derives from 'moon'. The moon is, of course, at the root of Monday, too – the day of the moon in most European languages. The pre-Christian *dies solaris* is only 'Sunday' in the unholy north, whereas it is the day of the Lord (*domenica* in Italian) around the Mediterranean. All our other days are named after pagan gods, highlighting how intertwined daily and religious life were, and also how Norse mythology liberally borrowed from the Greeks and Romans. In true heathen fashion, like our Teutonic ancestors, we still use capital letters for the days of the week and for the months, whereas Romance language speakers have desanctified and demoted the pagan gods to lower case.

In 321 AD the seven-day week was introduced by Emperor Constantine, a Christian, who, fed up with the ridiculous calends, ides and nones, may have either taken inspiration from Genesis or from the seven planets known at that time.

Most languages have no equivalent of 'weekend'. In French it is *le week-end*. France adopted *la semaine anglaise* in 1914 when their own *banques et des maisons de commerce* also decided to shut on Saturdays. 'Weekend' is one of the few English words that has entered the French language without too much protest, possibly because of its happy leisurely connotations. Initial Gallic re-spellings such as *ouiquende* soon disappeared, but in French Quebec *fin de semaine* is still battling it out with 'weekend'. The word *semaine* itself (Italian *settimana*) is simply based on the Latin for seven – *septimus*. In Sri Lanka in addition to the weekend, the full moon day (*Poya day*) is a holiday. On this day all places of entertainment are closed and no alcohol is on sale.

1 Markets, gods and planets

- Brainstorm to find out how many different parts of the day students can think of in English (e.g. sunrise, dawn, morning, dusk, etc.). Get them to define exactly what a day is – a period of light or a period of 24 hours or a working period (Did you have a good day at work?).

- Now brainstorm on the origin of the names of the days of the week in students' own languages.

- Students read the text and table for interest.

Follow-up 1

- In groups students imagine that they are part of a commission which has decided to abandon the seven-day week in favour of a three, four, five or ten-day week. They should analyse the pros and cons of each solution before making a final decision. Groups can then compare their decisions.

Follow-up 2

- In multinational groups students can compare the mnemonics they use for remembering the number of days in a month. In English we say: Thirty days has September, April, June and November. All the rest have thirty-one, save February which has twenty-eight.

A quick note on spelling

Students of all levels have problems with Tuesday and Thursday, either because they mix them up or because they can't spell them. Tuesday is the second day of the week, so tell students to remember it as *two's* day. Thursday is the fourth day, and the last two letters of 'four' are UR (plus *four's* day sounds very like *Thor's* day – see the table on the Students' Page).

1

MARKETS, GODS AND PLANETS

The seven-day week originated in west Asia, spread to Europe and later to north Africa. In other parts of Africa, three, four, five, six and eight-day weeks are found. The number of days corresponds to the number of different markets on different days in an area; in fact, the Congo word for 'week' is the same as for 'market'.

Not all languages have special names for the days of the week – in many other African languages, for example Swahili, they simply say 'first day', 'second day', etc. However, their first day doesn't always correspond to our first day, and is often Saturday. Most ancient civilisations – Egyptian, Babylonian, Mayan, Chinese, etc. – didn't have a concept of the week. Instead they had cycles of days, twenty days for the Mayans and Aztecs, rather than the European seven.

The English and German names of the week days derive from Scandinavia (see the third column in the table below), where originally a five-day week was used. The Scandinavians actually based their mythology on Greek and Roman mythology – so Woden and Mercury were both gods of war, and Frigg and Venus both goddesses of love. Today in Iceland, Sweden and Denmark, Saturday is still known as 'bath day' (*Laugardagur, Loerdag*), because some tribes were unable to find a Teutonic equivalent of the Romans' honouring of Saturn – the god of agriculture. The problem was resolved when they noticed the Roman soldiers' habit of taking a bath on this day!

Days of the week				
German	**English**	**planet/god/goddess**	**Latin**	**French**
Montag	Monday	Moon day	lunae dies	lundi
Dienstag	Tuesday	Twi's day (war)	dies Martis	mardi
Mittwoch	Wednesday	Woden (war, the dead)	dies Mercurii	mercredi
Donnerstag	Thursday	Thor (thunder)	dies Iovis	jeudi
Freitag	Friday	Frigg/Freya (love)	dies Veneris	vendredi
Samstag	Saturday	Saturn's day	Saturni/sambati dies	samedi
Sonntag	Sunday	Sun day	dies solaris (Dominus)	dimanche

2 The Sabbath

- Ask Christian, Muslim and Jewish students on which day the Sabbath is. This should lead into hypothesising on why Christians celebrate the Sabbath on a Sunday rather than a Saturday.

- Hand out photocopies and see if students know any of the answers to the nine questions, and then proceed to the listening.

Listening

- Students hear the answers to the nine questions.

1 Saturday.

  2 In the 4th century AD.

  3 Day of the sun, day of the lord.

  4 To commemorate Jesus' resurrection.

  5 Travel on horseback.

  6 For not going to church.

  7 Rabbits.

  8 1878.

  9 Six days, twelve hours a day.

A Now last week you told us about the origins of the days of the week. This evening I thought you might like to tell us about the weekend. I mean has the idea of the weekend always existed?

B Well, there's traditionally always been a day of rest. The Sabbath.

A But isn't the Sabbath a Saturday? I mean I know the Italian and Spanish words for Saturday sound very like 'Sabbath'.

B That's true, but back in the fourth century AD, the Roman emperor Constantine decided that Sunday should be a day of rest. And he changed the original Latin name, *dies solis*, which means 'day of the sun', to *dies di dominica* which means 'day of the lord'.

A 'Lord' as in 'God'?

B No, the 'lord' meant 'Jesus', since the day was supposed to commemorate his resurrection, which had of course been on a Sunday.

A And presumably the Christians wanted to distinguish themselves from the Jews by having their day of rest on a different day?

B Maybe. But in any case in Great Britain they passed all kinds of laws telling you what you could and could not do on a Sunday. For example, in the eighth century servants were not allowed to travel on horseback on a Sunday, but if slaves were made to work, then their masters had to pay a hefty fine. In Elizabeth the first's time you also had to pay a big fine if you didn't go to church. Then in the seventeenth and eighteenth centuries they introduced other bizarre laws about bakers, and fishing, and hunting. For example you weren't allowed to hunt game – deer, pheasants or what have you – but you could kill rabbits.

A But in any case, Sunday was still the first day of the week?

B Right.

A But how could it be both the first day of the week and part of the weekend too?

B Well, the idea of having a weekend is only quite recent. It was the result of some labour laws, from around 1878, which introduced a five-day working week. Until that time people had been slogging away down the mines, in factories and sweatshops for ten to twelve hours a day, six days a week. 'Weekend' soon became an international rallying word as other countries too wanted better working conditions.

A One final question. Does everyone in the world now have a weekend?

3 Thank God it's Friday

- Ask students, in groups, to decide which is the best day of the week and why.

- Hopefully some students will come up with Friday. Ask them if Friday has any special significance in their culture. Let them read the text for interest.

- Then ask them to stay in their groups and try to solve the puzzles. Give them not more than a couple of minutes and then get class feedback and give the answers.

1 The friend whispered 'Change horses.'

  2 It was the middle of the day.

- Students then discuss the questions on their page.

2 The Sabbath

1 When was the original Sabbath – Saturday or Sunday?

2 When did the Roman emperor Constantine decide to change the day of rest?

3 What do *dies solis* and *dies di dominica* mean?

4 Why was the day of rest changed?

5 What couldn't English servants in the eighth century do on a Sunday?

6 During the reign of Elizabeth I why might you be fined on a Sunday?

7 Which of these animals were you allowed to kill in Britain on a Sunday in the 18th century? rabbits, deer, pheasants

8 When was the five-day working week introduced into Britain:
1668   1678   1868   1878?

9 Until that date how many days a week did people work and for how many hours a day?

3 Thank God it's Friday

Friday is an important day in many religions – for some it is the last day of the week and is known as 'the day of assembly'. Christians associate Friday with fasting and eating fish; and with bad luck because of the connection with Christ's crucifixion. For the Jews sundown on Friday is the beginning of their Sabbath. Muslims are encouraged to go to the Mosque for all their prayers, but particularly on a Friday. Friday is also the last day of the working week for people in most countries of the world, thus many people have had to adapt their religious routines to fit in with the business week of the western world.

Friday afternoon is a time when students are winding down for the weekend.
Here are two puzzles for you to solve.

1 Two Irishmen who were mad about racing decided to have a horse race, but being Irish, they thought they would change the rules a little. It was decided that the man whose horse crossed the line last, rather than first, would be the winner. So they got on their horses, set off, and of course when they got near the finishing line they came to a halt and got off their horses. They stayed there a couple of days, they were rather stubborn by nature, and wondered how they would ever finish the race. Luckily a friend of theirs came along, heard what the problem was, and then whispered something to both of them. They immediately mounted and galloped as fast as they could towards the finishing line. What did their friend whisper?

2 An extremely black African American, dressed entirely in black, with his eyes and mouth shut, is walking down the middle of a tarmacked road in Harlem which has no streetlamps. There is no light coming from any of the buildings which are all painted black. A black car with no headlights on is coming down the road, which has no markings. Despite all this the car manages to avoid hitting the man. How or why?

1 Do you enjoy solving puzzles like these? What kind of mental abilities are required?

2 Do you have any equivalents of Irish jokes and stories?

3 Is it acceptable to make fun of other nationalities? Why? Why not?

4 What kind of jokes are not acceptable in your culture?

5 Who is the best joke teller in your class?

6 What do you do when you don't understand a joke?

7 Do jokes translate well from one language to another? Why? Why not?

Appendix

Day 7

In Great Britain, Mother's Day is celebrated on the fourth Sunday in Lent. The church called it *Dominica Refectionis*, the Sunday of refreshments, as people could have a temporary break from fasting. It used to be know as *Mothering Sunday* since people in villages went to the mother-church of their parish to offer gifts; and girls, who were working as servants, used to go home and take gifts (flowers or simnel cake) for their mothers. During the Second World War, US servicemen in Britain mistook Mothering Sunday for their own Mother's Day, held on the second Sunday in May – this led to a kind of amalgamation of the two days. In the US, Congress adopted Mother's Day in 1913 following campaigning by Anna Jarvis of Philadelphia, who lost her own mother in 1907, and initiated church services and the wearing of carnations (red for a living mother, white for a dead one). Today in the US and UK people celebrate their mothers by sending them flowers, cards or phoning them. In fact more long distance phone calls are made in the USA on this day than on any other day.

Day 8

1 Fundamentalists believe that the world was created in 4004 BC (on October 22). 47% of Americans believe God created man within the last 10,000 years.

2 See Genesis 4.15–24 for the expulsion from the Garden of Eden story and Genesis 5 to see just how long the first people on earth lived. (Apparently the earth's population grew rapidly because of human longevity – Methuselah holds the record of 969 years.) In 1996 Pope John Paul II declared that evolution is 'more than just a theory' and is fully compatible with the Christian faith. But, while the human body may have evolved gradually, the soul 'is immediately created by God' in each person. Back in 1950 Pope Pius XII had already called evolution a 'serious hypothesis', and, as early as the 5th century, St Augustine had warned against a too literal reading of the creation story. One nice explanation I heard from a Mormon was that, indeed, the world was created in seven days, but just how long those days were is a matter of speculation, in the sense that a biblical day could have been a million years.

3 My English Bible says this event took place in 2448 BC. *The Ryrie Study Bible** gives the following information about Noah's ark: "A vessel of such dimensions [i.e. those described in Genesis 6] would have a displacement of about 20,000 tons and gross tonnage of about 14,000 tons. Its carrying capacity equaled that of 522 standard railroad stock cars (each of which can hold 240 sheep). Only 188 cars would be required to hold 45,000 sheep-sized animals, leaving three trains of 104 cars each for food, Noah's family, and 'range' for the animals. Today it is estimated that there are 17,600 kinds of animals, making 45,000 a likely approximation of the number Noah might have taken into the ark."

At the time of writing, a heated court case is taking place in Australia concerning the existence of the ark. Several archaeologists have been hoodwinking fundamentalists into giving them money to excavate for the ark while really pursuing their own ends. But led on by this, one Christian fundamentalist leader has claimed to have found the site of the ark, against hard scientific evidence that the myth has its roots in the great flooding in Iraq around 2600 BC, which is also mentioned in the Mithraic religion in the Book of Gilgamesh (which also contains a resurrection story – see the notes to Day 26: Winter Solstice).

4 See Exodus 20 for the ten commandments, and Leviticus 20–23 for some fascinating laws. (This is a must for anyone interested in ancient laws regarding food and sex.) The Jewish festival Shabuot celebrates the day God gave Moses the ten commandments.

5 See Luke 1. 29–39: Then Mary said unto the angel, 'How shall this be, seeing I know not a man?' And the angel answered and said unto her, 'The Holy Ghost shall come upon thee, and the power of the Highest shall overshadow thee; therefore also that holy thing which shall be born of thee shall be called the Son of God.' The Immaculate Conception refers to Mary being born without sin.

6 For example: shrivelled hand (Luke 6.6–11); back from the dead (Luke 7.13); feeding the five thousand (Luke 9.16–17).

7 68% of Britons consider themselves Christian and 50% believe in the Resurrection.

* Taken from *The Ryrie Study Bible* by Dr Charles Ryrie.
Copyright 1976, Moody Bible Institute of Chicago, IL USA.
Moody Press. Used by permission.

Day 13

Listening 2

A I know that in Sweden, for example, fathers are actively encouraged to spend time with their new children, they're paid to take time off work, in order to spend yeah months at a time.

B So who pays for it?

A The government. The government. [Oh right] I don't know if the same is true in France.

C They're trying to do it more and more here where they are. Some some companies are trying to be kind of daddy friendly, and giving paternity leave, but it's completely at the discretion of the company, so I think maybe here the company must pay for it. [yeah] But it's a shame, you know, because also the mum needs the daddy there [yeah right yeah].

B Yeah well in an ideal world, yes, great, it would be lovely if you had the the father there, but I don't think it works in ... It it obviously it differs from country to country. The different cultural ... Think of somewhere like Greece, where I've spent some time, and um the father's role is that of going out and working to provide for the family, and the mother is essentially the one that brings the children up [well, I think, yes, I think apart from the ...] they don't wash up. [No certainly not.] They come home 'Where's my food?'

D Apart from the, you know, a couple of countries really, like Germany, the Scandinavian countries, and maybe America slightly now, everywhere else is exactly as you say, I mean it's a terribly traditional way of looking at the family.

C It's actually quite a sexist way of looking at the family.

A And short-sighted, I think, too.

B Well, how long has it been like this though? Um I mean the new father thing that you say, I mean do you imagine that in Scandinavia that's been going on for more than 20 years?

A Well, it's ... I the reason I mention that it's short-sighted is that obviously it's countries who are thinking about the long term future of their countries and thinking about the education of their children. And the kind of society that they want their kids to live in [twenty years down the road].

C Well, society is changing now. I mean it has to change because women are more and more going out to work, not just out of necessity, but a lot of the time from choice, so it's got to be a two-way job for bringing up children.

Day 19

ⓘ

Maps at this time generally showed the world as being flat. We don't know who first had the idea that the earth was a sphere. Aristotle, the Greek philosopher, reasoned that since a sphere was a perfect mathematical shape, it was the perfect shape to represent the earth and the universe. He also pointed out that in a lunar eclipse, when the moon moves into the Earth's shadow, the edge of the shadow is circular.

Knowledge of the Earth's spherical shape was not taught in schools but was the possession of a few academics. Interest in the Earth's shape was renewed by the Spanish and Portuguese who were blocked by Moslems from exploiting the riches of India. They wanted to know whether they could reach India by sailing west, thus the real shape of the Earth became very important. Even in Columbus' time intelligent people thought the world was flat, and it took a lot of convincing by Columbus that his ship would not fall off the edge of the world.

The expedition of the Portuguese navigator, Ferdinand Magellan, was the first to complete the circumnavigation of the Earth (1519–22).

Day 22

Songs for our ancestors

The ancestors have spoken today

Kwaro tin dong oloko;
Uyeny nyok kibworo,
Gweno ki kongo.
Wora, ceng ikoko cam,
Cammi tin en;
Bin iye dong;
Lwong omegini ducu;
Camwu en.

The ancestors have spoken today;
Bring forth a brown billy goat,
chicken and beer.
My father, you have asked for food;
Your food is here today;
Come to it now;
Call all your brothers,
Your food is here.

You, our fathers,
Accept the food we give you today;
Let your children have good health;
Let the women have good childbirth.
So that your name may not be obliterated.

Okot p'Bitek, Uganda

For Joe Mackinaw

In my youth
I went south,
In my dreams
I went south

There
I watched them hunt ...
I watched them hunt the buffalo.
And in my heart
I hunted with them.

Now they are gone.
The buffalo have left,
Ashamed,
That we had let them die,
Mercilessly,
At the hands of the white hunters.

Jim Dumont, Canadian Indian

The Past

Let no one say the past is dead.
The past is all about us and within.
Haunted by tribal memories, I know
This little now, this accidental present
Is not the all of me, whose long making
Is so much of the past ...
A thousand thousand camp fires in the forest
Are in my blood.
Let none tell me the past is wholly gone.
Now is so small a part of time, so small a part
Of all the race years that have moulded me.

Oodgeroo Noonuccal, Australian aborigine

Untitled

in
dian

we are north americans
he said
and made me feel
ashamed
that i was not wearing
beads at my throat
small proud flowers
growing there
or leather
sarain stump
handsome faced
colour of earth rose
quietly telling me that i am
indian now
and ending all
the identity fears

Skyros Bruce, Canadian Indian

Day 26

The pagan 'Yule' is the origin of the word for Christmas in many nordic countries: *Jul* in Danish, Swedish and Norwegian plus Finnish *Joulua* and Estonian *Joulu*. In Gaelic languages the words for Christmas (*Nadolig, Nollaig, Nodlog*) all derive from the Latin *natalica* (nativity). A similar root is for *Natale, Noël* etc., which come from the Latin *dies natalis* (birthday, originally *dies natalis invicti solis*, birthday of the unconquered sun, with reference to Mithras and the ancient sun-God Attis).

Day 27

Christmas quiz

 The languages are:

  a Boas Festas – Portuguese

  b Buon Natale – Italian

  c Feliz Navidad – Spanish

  d Fröhliche Weihnachten – German

  e Gajan Kristnaskon – Esperanto

  f Glaedelig Jul – Danish

  g Hristos se rodi – Serbian

  h Joyeux Noël – French

  i Nadolig Llawen – Welsh

  j Selamat Hari Krisna, Dan Tahun Bahru – Malay

Christmas games

 1 Spot the difference

In the picture on page 88...:

  1 There is no fairy on the Christmas tree.

  2 There are only six presents under the tree.

  3 Two children are opening presents.

  4 One of the people at the table is different.

  5 The turkey has not been eaten.

  6 The candles are not lit.

  7 The Christmas cards are on the wall.

  8 The fire is not lit.

  9 There is no mistletoe.

  10 There is no Christmas pudding.

Answers

3 1 incorrectly   **2** A hole.   **3** Your name.   **4** A bald head.

4 He was a night watchman, so he shouldn't have been asleep dreaming.

5 First move the top coin and put it under the row of four coins, between the second and third coins. Now take the first and fourth coins in the row of four coins, and put them on either side of the coins on what was originally the second row. And hey presto!

Day 27

Carols

The word 'carol' either comes from the Latin *choraula* (a flute player) via the old French *carole* or is of Celtic origin (in Breton a *koroll* was a dance, in old Cornish a *carol* was a choir or a concert, and in Welsh it meant a song). In any case they've been around for at least 1000 years, though the first printed collection was published in 1521.

Away in a Manger

Away in a manger, no crib for a bed,
The little Lord Jesus laid down his sweet head;
The stars in the bright sky looked down where he lay,
The little Lord Jesus asleep on the hay.

The cattle are lowing, the baby awakes,
But little Lord Jesus, no crying he makes;
I love thee, Lord Jesus: look down from the sky
And stay by my side until morning is nigh.

Be near me, Lord Jesus: I ask thee to stay
Close by me for ever, and love me I pray;
Bless all the dear children in thy tender care
And fit us for heaven, to live with thee there.

Traditional

We Wish You a Merry Christmas

We wish you a merry Christmas
We wish you a merry Christmas
We wish you a merry Christmas
And a happy New Year.

We want some figgy pudding
We want some figgy pudding
We want some figgy pudding
And a cup of good cheer.

We won't go until we get some
We won't go until we get some
We won't go until we get some
So bring it out here!

We wish you a merry Christmas
We wish you a merry Christmas
We wish you a merry Christmas
And a happy New Year.

Traditional

Jingle Bells

Dashing through the snow
In a one-horse open sleigh
Through the fields we go
Laughing all the way.
Bells on bob-tail ring
Making spirits bright
What fun it is to ride and sing
A sleighing song tonight.

Jingle bells, jingle bells
Jingle all the way,
Oh what fun it is to ride
In a one-horse open sleigh, O
Jingle bells, jingle bells
Jingle all the way,
Oh what fun it is to ride
In a one-horse open sleigh.

John Parpont (1859)

Good King Wenceslas

Good King Wenceslas looked out on the feast of Stephen.
When the snow lay round about, deep and crisp and even.
Brightly shone the moon that night, though the frost was cruel,
When a poor man came in sight, gathering winter fuel.

Hither page and stand by me, if thou knowst it telling
Yonder peasant, who is he, where and what his dwelling?
Sire, he lives a good league hence, underneath the mountain,
Right against the forest fence, by Saint Agnes' fountain.

Bring me flesh and bring me wine, bring me pinelogs hither
Thou and I will see him dine when we bear them thither.
Page and monarch forth they went, forth they went together
Through the rude wind's wild lament, and the bitter weather.

Sire the night is darker now, and the wind blows stronger
Fails my heart I know not how, I can go no longer.
Mark my footsteps my good page, tread thou in them boldly
Thou shalt find the winter's rage freeze thy blood less coldly.

In his master's steps he trod where the snow lay dinted
Heat was in the very sod which the saint had printed
Therefore Christian men be sure, wealth or rank possessing,
Ye who now will bless the poor, shall yourselves find blessing.

Traditional

Twelve Days of Christmas

On the (first) day of Christmas my true love sent to me
Twelve lords leaping
Eleven ladies dancing
Ten pipers piping
Nine drummers drumming
Eight maids milking
Seven swans swimming
Six geese laying
Five gold rings
Four colly birds
Three french hens
Two turtle doves and
A partridge in a pear tree

Traditional

Silent Night

Silent night! Holy night!
All is calm, all is bright,
Round yon virgin mother and child;
Holy infant, so tender and mild,
　　Sleep in heavenly peace,
　　Sleep in heavenly peace.

Silent night! Holy night!
Shepherds quail at the sight;
Glories stream from heaven afar,
Heavenly hosts sing Alleluia!
　　Christ the Saviour is born.
　　Christ the Saviour is born.

Silent night! Holy night!
Son of God, love's pure light
Radiant beams from thy holy face,
With the dawn of redeeming grace,
　　Jesus, Lord, at thy birth,
　　Jesus, Lord, at thy birth.

Joseph Mohr

Translated by John Freeman Young

The Holly and The Ivy

The holly and the ivy,
When they are both full-grown,
Of all the trees that are in the wood,
The holly bears the crown.
The rising of the sun
And the running of the deer
The playing of the merry organ,
Sweet singing in the choir.

The holly bears a blossom
As white as lily flower,
And Mary bore sweet Jesus Christ
To be our sweet Saviour.

The holly bears a berry
As red as any blood,
And Mary bore sweet Jesus Christ
To do poor sinners good.

The holly bears a prickle
As sharp as any thorn,
And Mary bore sweet Jesus Christ
On Christmas Day in the morn.

The holly bears a bark
As bitter as any gall,
And Mary bore sweet Jesus Christ
For to redeem us all.

Traditional

Day 28

Personality Profile

Some of your aspirations tend to be pretty unrealistic. At times you are extroverted, affable, sociable, while at other times you are introverted, wary and reserved. You have found it unwise to be too frank in revealing yourself to others. You pride yourself on being an independent thinker and do not accept others' opinions without satisfactory proof. You prefer a certain amount of change and variety, and become dissatisfied when hemmed in by restrictions and limitations. At times you have serious doubts as to whether you have made the right decision or done the right thing.

Day 28

Listening 1

1 My name is Anne Ray. I was born on 29 May 1952 in Whitehaven in Cumbria. my star sign is Gemini, which is the twin sign. Typically Geminis are known for starting things but not finishing them. I don't think this is typical of me because, although I do like to start lots of things and I have lots of things going on, I do tend to finish whatever I start.

2 My name is Timothy Mitchell. I was born in Fort Worth, Texas, of course, in the United States on August 12 1971. My zodiac sign or my star sign would be Leo and some of the characteristics of Leo would be, a Leo would be a born leader. I don't know if I'm a born leader, but I'm not really a follower. As far as more characteristics – pride and dignity – I think I have very much so, I'm very much prideful about what I do as far as work and every day going ons and then in my life.

3 My name is Jean Quick. I was born in Manchester on November 19 1926. I'm a Scorpio. I'm a typical Scorpio because I say what I think and I'm exceedingly sociable.

4 My name is Gillian Brogdon. I was born in Cambridge on 1 May 1954. My zodiac sign is Taurus and, although I don't particularly believe in horoscopes, some of the things are quite relevant to me, particularly liking good food, because I'm a cook, so I do like good food. And also I'm attached to family and friends, which is also quite relevant.

5 My name is Anna Southern. I was born on 25 September 1972. I'm from Rochdale in Lancashire. My star sign is Libra. They say that Librans are very indecisive, but I'm not really into horoscopes, so I don't know whether I believe that.

Day 28

Listening 2

A Welcome to this special birthday edition of *One World*. Yes, folks, we've been on the air for exactly one year now, and we thought it would be a nice idea to have a special programme dedicated to birthday celebrations around the world. With us in the studio tonight we have Shaheen Haq, and Pat Cane, who has a weekly column on birthdays in the *Toronto Daily Star*.

B Good evening.

C Good evening.

A Shaheen, perhaps we could begin with you. How are birthdays celebrated in India?

B Well, I think perhaps we're all assuming that everyone in the world celebrates their birthday. This just isn't the case. Low income families in India, for instance, simply can't afford any festivities. And most Muslims don't celebrate their birthdays.

C I think Shaheen has raised an interesting point here. The Christian church, too, was actively against celebrating birthdays, and in any case most people, until a couple of hundred years ago, they couldn't even read and wouldn't have even been able to spot their birthday on a calendar anyway.

B Of course some Muslims do celebrate their birthdays. In Egypt, Turkey and Indonesia, for example, the rich people invite friends and families around. But not in the small villages.

A Here in England your twenty-first is the big one. Is that true of other countries too?

C Actually the British seem to be fairly unique on that one. I mean in most of the West eighteen is the most important birthday. In Finland, just to name one typical example, eighteen is the age when you can vote, you know, or buy wines, drive a car and so on. But in Japan I think you have to wait till you're twenty before you can smoke or drink.

B I know in Senegal, which is another predominantly Muslim country, girls get to vote at sixteen and boys at eighteen. And in Bangladesh, girls at eighteen and boys at twenty-one.

A That's interesting. I mean is that typical that around the world girls are considered to be more mature than boys?

B Yes, I think it is, and there are some countries, particularly in South America, which only have a big party for the girls. In Mexico and Argentina, for example, they have enormous parties for 15-year-old girls.

C As a kind of coming out into society?

B Yes, it's to celebrate when you become a woman. [Right] You have a really big party. Your parents buy you a really nice dress, and invite all the family and your friends. All the neighbours give you presents. And in some places the partying goes on for days, even weeks, I've been told.

C You know in Norway they have a great party for anyone who's not married by the time they're thirty. It's kind of embarrassing. I mean you get pepper thrown at you.

A Pepper? Why pepper?

C I'm not really sure.

B So does that mean that on your twenty-ninth birthday you can start thinking 'God I better get married.'

C Well, I'm not sure how seriously they take it.

A In England we have quite big parties for your fortieth, fiftieth, sixtieth and so on.

C Well in Japan your eighty-eighth is considered ...

A Eighty-eighth?

C ... to be the luckiest birthday. Eight is a very lucky number in Japan.